The Making of the 20th Century

This series of specially commissioned titles focuses attention on significant and often controversial events and themes of world history in the present century. The authors, many of them already outstanding in their field, have tried to close the gap between the intelligent layman, whose interest is aroused by recent history, and the specialist student at university. Each book will therefore provide sufficient narrative and explanation for the newcomer while offering the specialist student detailed source-references and bibliographies, together with interpretation and reassessment in the light of recent scholarship.

In the choice of subjects there will be a balance between breadth in some spheres and detail in others; between the essentially political and matters scientific, economic or social. The series cannot be a comprehensive account of everything that has happened in the twentieth century, but it will provide a guide to recent research and explain something of the times of extraordinary change and complexity in which we live.

The Making of the 20th Century

Series Editor: CHRISTOPHER THORNE

Titles in the Series include

The Human Consequences of Urbanisation

DIVERGENT PATHS IN THE URBAN
EXPERIENCE OF THE TWENTIETH
CENTURY

Brian J. L. Berry

Irving B. Harris Professor of Urban Geography
The University of Chicago

St. Martin's Press   New York

FOR **JAN**

Contents

The illustration on the front of the jacket is an aerial photograph
of Letchworth, Hertfordshire. Reproduced with the permission of
the Radio Times–Hulton Picture Library.

Acknowledgements

I AM indebted to many people for their critical reviews of earlier drafts of the manuscript that ultimately became this book. But for the sandpapering I received from them, the book would have been very rough-hewn. In particular, I wish to acknowledge my debt to Janet Abu-Lughod, John Adams, Robert McC. Adams, William Alonso, Douglas Caruso, Michael Dear, Roger Downs, Allison Dunham, John Dyckman, Dennis Fair, Claude Fischer, Jack Fisher, John Friedmann, Peter Goheen, Steven Golant, Peter Gould, Scott Greer, Peter Hall, Niles Hansen, Chauncy Harris, Doris Holleb, John Kasarda, Robert Lake, Nathaniel Lithwick, Akin Mabogunge, Harold McKinney, Jack Meltzer, William Miner, Derick Mirfin, Manning Nash, John Osman, Ferenc Probald, John Seley, Arie Shachar, Milton Singer, Howard Spodek, Gerald Suttles, Harry Swain, Christopher Thorne, Peter Tyson, Paul Wheatley, Julian Wolpert, Marshall Worden, and Melvin Webber. In addition, those who contributed their technical skills should be recognised. Douglas Cargo put in many hours redrafting the illustrations, Quentin Gillard prepared the index, and Mary Grear typed the manuscript.

A final and special word of thanks must go to my wife. That I could spend the time I did travelling, writing and rewriting, I owe to Janet, who has been the foundation making it possible.

B. J. L. B.

Park Forest, Illinois
January 1973

Preface

WHEN Christopher Thorne asked me to fill the gap that had emerged in his series because of the untimely death of the distinguished British sociologist John Madge, I agreed with reluctance. A book with a prescribed title, *The Human Consequences of Urbanisation*, to be of no more than sixty thousand words, in a series devoted to 'The Making of the 20th Century', is hardly the obvious thing to be written by a person whose early career had been devoted to 'quantitative' geography, despite a sometime education in economics and political science, on-the-job training in urban sociology, and a practical yen for urban and regional planning. As it turned out, this combination of interests was to stand me in good stead. I had no idea that I would take more than a year longer than promised to write the book. Nor did I realise that this would be a period in which my concerns with national policy and social change would finally crystallise or that the period spent re-shaping an initial rough draft would be one of unique opportunity.

During recent years my several lives as a professional geographer, lecturer on urbanism and planning consultant have taken me into every continent and many of the world's major cities, save only China, the U.S.S.R. and North Africa. On these trips I had the opportunity to work with policy makers, urban and regional analysts and planners, as well as the chance to see and to smell the many forms of city in the world today.

One thing became clear in these travels. I should not write a highly technical, narrowly professional essay in my usual 'mathematicised' manner. Rather, I should be responsive to a clearly felt need throughout the world for a general overview of the substantive and ideological aspects of twentieth-century urbanisation and its human consequences. The need was all the more pressing because I saw planners throughout the world attempting to stem the growth of the largest cities in order to produce 'balanced' urbanisation and to create more humane urban environments within the framework of a particular conventional wisdom, while at the same time I saw increasing numbers of citizens growing alarmed because the plans were not working.

As I travelled, I perceived that the intellectual basis for much urban policy was derived from social theories written about *nineteenth*-century urbanisation. I thus came to appreciate that many of the difficulties being experienced stemmed from a simple fact : *the conventional wisdom was no longer valid*. The opportunity to compare a variety of circumstances around the world in rapid succession also convinced me that, despite certain broad commonalities, there was not one but *several* paths being taken by twentieth-century urbanisation, and that both the causes and the human consequences differed along these paths. Many of the world's practical urbanists are now coming to realise the need for new intellectual frameworks specifically applicable to different socio-political circumstances.

Thus, what I do in this book is to disavow the view that urbanisation is a universal process, a consequence of modernisation that involves the same sequence of events in different countries and that produces progressive convergence of forms. Nor do I subscribe to the view that there may be several culturally specific processes, but that they are producing convergent results because of underlying technological imperatives of modernisation and industrialisation. I feel very strongly not only that we are dealing with several fundamentally different processes that have arisen out of differences in culture and time, but also that these processes are producing different results in different world regions, transcending any superficial similarities.

It would have been easy to write a focused and highly disciplined report on a piece of analysis undertaken as if the single-process theory that informs conventional wisdom obtained. But to do this would have been both intellectually dishonest and unresponsive to the needs around the world as I saw them. I elected to follow the much more difficult path of marshalling and codifying evidence from a wide range of sources and interpreting this evidence in light of my own observations and experiences in ways that I hope will both challenge the specialist and inform the general reader.

The initial chapter deals with the conventional wisdom, the

base of social theory against which the twentieth-century materials may be judged. An examination of the nature of the nineteenth-century industrial urbanisation provides the backdrop for considering the succession of major works written about the social transformation that took place in these cities, the popular social movements that arose, and the emergence of urban planning as a reaction against some of the most deleterious effects of cities on health and social life.

Chapter 2 follows with a detailed examination of the North American experience. There are several reasons I discuss North America first and in most detail. Most obviously, it is the case I know best, and thus, without apology, I take advantage of this fact to develop the theories used in later chapters. But more importantly, significant changes have taken place and are taking place in North America that are as yet little understood elsewhere in the world, where there remains a tendency to use an image of what the American city became in the mid-twentieth century—but, parenthetically, is no longer—as an idealised picture (or spectre) of what cities elsewhere ought to or might become. It was in North America that much of the traditional social theory of the human consequences of urbanisation was codified by the Chicago School of urban sociologists in the inter-war period. The North American experience was also dominated by rapid economic and technological change, relatively unfettered by public intervention, which might lend some credence to use of the American experience as a lesson for urban policy makers elsewhere. But these changes produced first one new form of city, the decentralised metropolis of the automobile era, and more recently a second and totally new form of urban region that is secondary to both national networks of interdependence and the intensification of local cultures and life styles. In these new circumstances, the conventional social theory has been tested and found wanting, and it may even be questioned whether 'urbanisation' or 'the city' remain as relevant categories for analysis. What I do in the second part of the chapter is to try to develop the bases of an alternative theory applicable to these new conditions in America today.

The third chapter deals with the Third World, because conventional theorists have said it is there that one should expect a repetition of the nineteenth-century experience of the West as modernisation has diffused and urbanisation has taken place. This

The U.S. city model does not fit the 3rd world.

thesis is explored and found wanting. The baseline cultures are different, the pace of urban growth is faster, and different links exist between urban growth and the socio-political circumstances in which it is taking place. The result is new forms of cities and a totally new array of social conditions. Yet, in the Third World, western-educated policy makers have been grappling with urbanisation using the nineteenth-century model and proposing alien solutions either consistent with or in reaction to that model. Their policies seldom have the predicted consequences, whichever of the two routes is taken.

The fourth chapter then turns to the several European experiences, involving paths that differ from the industrial urbanisation of the West during the nineteenth century and from those of North America and the Third World in the twentieth century. The differences arise because of the varying mixtures of technological change, national ideologies and planning powers in the different European nations. In combination, such mixtures have created significantly different forms of urbanisation in which there are diverging human consequences.

This discussion of the European experience is delayed to Chapter 4 for a very specific reason. Neither existing theory nor conventional wisdom capture the several processual streams in the world today, particularly those streams that embody attempts, delicate and otherwise, to engineer social change to achieve explicit goals. This is even more the case when the goals are fashioned out of reactions *against* the perceived human consequences of nineteenth-century industrial urbanisation, as they were in most parts of Europe. Thus, it is toward the shaping of new bodies of theory incorporating these new variables that the volume leads, and it is the European experience that contributes most to the attempt.

Given the European evidence, the final chapter seeks to interpret the urbanisation processes that characterise different socio-political situations in the world today in terms of the public planning styles that are assumed in these contexts. Thus, North American urbanisation is seen as being driven by both a technological and a social dynamic under conditions of competitive bargaining and interest-group politics. The public interest is expressed in a reactive and conservative manner, designed to reduce the problems that arise as the powerful economic forces of mainstream America run their course. In spite of many attempts to do otherwise, Third World urbanisation is also seen to be the product of an unconstrained dynamic, for public powers have been swamped by the scale and pace of change in spite of highly centralised and increasingly authoritarian governmental forms. That Third World urbanisation is different from that of North America is to be attributed to different cultural contexts, to differential technological impacts, and in particular to the substitution, for the driving mainstream of self-interest, competitively exercised, of communal concerns, jointly expressed or publicly articulated. In Europe, on the other hand, there have been developed variously effective means of regulating urban change in the public interest, means of instituting public counterpoints to speculative private interests, and forms of explicitly directed urbanisation. In each of these cases the sought-after human consequences of urbanisation have become part of the urbanisation process through public intervention; directed change has contributed to a difference in outcomes, and in many cases these outcomes differ markedly from those predicted by the conventional wisdom.

Chiefly, Economic forces govern the U.S. city planning dynamics.

Chap. 1 — normative social theory (U.S.)
Chap. 2 — as applied to the American experience
Chap. 3 — ~~European~~ Third World socio-political circumstances
Chap. 4 — e.g. of 3rd World planning as embodying the cultural and sociological ~~characteristics~~ context of explored in Chap. 3
(incl. differences) consequences)

1 Nineteenth-Century Industrial Urbanisation

A NEW kind of city emerged during the nineteenth century, built on productive power, massed population and industrial technology. By the end of the century, this new city had been credited with the creation of a system of social life founded on entirely new principles. These principles, codified by a succession of social philosophers, were accepted as axiomatic by both academics and the public at large for the first half of the twentieth century. As new problems in the new cities produced a variety of social movements, the principles became the 'conventional wisdom' informing the public intervention that sought to correct the problems. In that intervention are to be found the roots of modern urban planning, which has sought to regulate or direct urbanisation in the twentieth century so as to change its human consequences. Thus, as a basis for understanding twentieth-century urbanisation, we must begin with the nineteenth-century experience. That is the purpose of this chapter.

'A MOST REMARKABLE SOCIAL PHENOMENON'

Where should we start? A baseline is needed. Such bases are rare in social science, so we are fortunate to have available Adna Ferrin Weber's masterpiece *The Growth of Cities in the Nineteenth Century* (1899). Weber's work was the first conceptually sound comprehensive statistical study of cities in the English language.

Weber, like many of his contemporaries, recognised that something dramatic had occurred during the nineteenth century. 'The most remarkable social phenomenon of the present century', he began, 'is the concentration of population in cities . . . The tendency towards concentration or agglomeration is all but universal in the Western world.' He then asked and sought answers to what remain the fundamental questions arising from these changes : What are the forces that have produced such a shifting of population? Are they enduring? What is to be the ultimate result? What are the economic, moral, political and social consequences of the redistribution of population? What is to be the attitude of the publicist, the statesman, the teacher toward the movement? 'They are not', he said,

questions capable of off-hand answers, for they are parts of a great problem which touches or underlies most of the practical questions of the day. The social problem that confronts practical people is in a very great degree the problem of the city. It is, therefore, of prime importance to ascertain the extent of the movement and its probable direction in the future; the forces that may be presumed to cause it; the more immediate as well as the ultimate consequences; and the possible remedies.

To this we can but agree, for seventy-five years later the questions remain of equal validity, even though new forces have been set in motion by the attempt to provide remedies. Just as Weber tried to provide answers relevant to his day, we will try to provide answers relevant to ours.

The Scale and Causes of Nineteenth-Century Urbanisation
Weber proceeded carefully and cautiously. Country by country, he probed the data available, questioning definitions and statistical reliability, seeking comparability. 'In order to bring statistics of urban population in different countries into comparison', he wrote, 'the author has aimed to secure, as the town unit, an actual agglomeration of people, and not a territorial unit or political subdivision.' Finally, he was able to produce a statistical summary for the nineteenth century.

Immediately, he said : 'One is impressed with the extent of the variations in the percentage of urban population in the different countries of the world', and he began to test a series of hypotheses that might help explain the variation. 'Of the causes of such extensive variation, that which most readily suggests itself is density of population.' But after examining the statistics, he concluded that there were evidently other factors producing agglomerations than mere populousness. What factors? Weber felt he could demonstrate that the Industrial Revolution and the era of railways, both of which opened earliest in England and the United States, were the transforming agents in the redistribution of population.

Later analysts, notably Simon Kuznets (1966), have confirmed

Weber's suppositions. Kuznets has shown that the salient features of nineteenth-century growth in the West were high rates of increase in per capita product (from 15 per cent to 30 per cent per decade), accompanied by substantial rates of population growth (over 10 per cent per decade). This meant very large increases in total product and great pressure on natural resources, and was accompanied by wide differentials in the rates on natural increase among different economic and social groups. This economic growth was due in large measure to improved production techniques. Only a small part of the increase came from increased inputs of labour, capital or natural resources. About one-fifth of the increase in per capita production came from increases in man hours or physical capital per worker. Primarily, the increase was due to improvements of the quality of the inputs, which meant essentially greater efficiency traceable to increases in useful knowledge and improved industrial organisation and institutional arrangements. All sectors of the modernising economies participated in the increasing efficiency. Agriculture, which generally has been the sector with the lowest increase, nonetheless had a significantly large increase. Transportation and communication generally had the largest increases, even larger than industry. Services had the lowest rates of increase.

Accompanying increasing efficiency were changes in the relative importance of the sectors, involving a decline in the share of agriculture, a rise in the share of manufacturing and public utilities, shifts within manufacturing from less to more desirable goods, an increase in the share of some service groups (personal, professional, government) and declines in others (domestic service), and shifts in the allocation of capital.

At the same time there were significant changes in the structure of final demand, both the cause and the effect of changes in the production process. Technological improvements and varying income elasticities of demand yielded complicated causal relationships that involved such changes as shifts in the regional allocation of resources, shifts in the share of labour in the different sectors of the economy, higher rates of expansion of foreign trade, and changes in the international division of labour.

Other changes included increases in the average size of production units, since there were marked and rapid shifts of product and labour from small towards larger firms and organisations. This occurred most visibly in manufacturing and public utilities, where improved technology generally involved larger capital investment and economies of scale. There was a related shift downward in relative importance from own-account to employee status, from small unincorporated units to large impersonal corporations, from self-employed or family employed to employee or worker status.

Finally, the shifts in capital allocation, in product and in labour, depended upon relatively rapid institutional adjustments and the mobility of factor inputs. For example, the shifts in final demand and in the division of labour often developed chain reactions that involved shifts in population and labour force, both geographically and by type. Considerable migration in space and occupation were required to adjust labour supply to changing demand and to the changing types of production units.

In short, then, nineteenth-century modernisation in the West involved a process whereby, as societies modernised, their market mechanisms expanded in scope and influence. The size of production units increased, as did the number and complexity of production decisions, and increasing scale and complexity produced impersonality in the use of services of others in transportation, communication, financing and policing.

Increased division of labour and increased specialisation, the necessary concomitants of increased productivity, inevitably became forces promoting population concentration in cities. Associated with this population shift, indeed an integral part of it, was the shift in the occupational structure of economies. Increased division of labour, increased markets, and increased urbanisation all required or resulted in shifts from agriculture and from unskilled occupations in primary production to more skilled clerical and 'high level' occupations, largely in urban concentrations. New institutions were created and old institutions were radically altered. This was particularly true in the case of financial and market institutions which, in turn, contributed to a massive accumulation of social and economic overhead in cities, making further high-level productivity increases possible and the modern institutions more effective. Thus, external economies built up after the initial periods of modernisation loosened traditional social structures, and contributed to further breakup of traditional patterns of economic behaviour, in increasingly complex cycles of mutual causation and interdependence.

Migration and Natural Increase

Weber's observations anticipated many of Kuznets' detailed ana-
lytic results. But Weber went further than Kuznets in probing
the human consequences of industrial urbanisation. Noting that
cityward migration fed the growth of the cities, he asked : What
were the features of the migration streams? Who migrated from
where to where, and why? Migration had to be separated from
natural increase of the population and from suburban annexa-
tions by cities, especially since during the nineteenth century
Weber found that cities had reversed their role. Earlier, they had
been 'destroyers of mankind' with substantial excesses of deaths
over births, but by the later years he was studying they were beginning to produce surpluses of births, although considerable
diversity existed from one country to another.

Careful statistical analysis enabled him to probe the nature of
cityward migration. It was clear to him that emigration was predominantly from agricultural areas. The migration streams flowed
towards manufacturing and commercial towns, and the bulk of the
migration was short distance. The demands for more labour in the
cities were met by the flocking in of the inhabitants immediately
surrounding the town; the gaps thus left in the rural population
were met by immigrants from more remote districts until the
attractive force of the rapidly growing city made its influence felt,
step by step, to the most remote corners of the country.

To any city, emigration from outlying areas was seen to decrease with distance. Weber also found that the distance travelled
by migrants varied in the same ratio as the magnitude of the city
which was their destination. The larger the town, the wider its
circle of influence in attracting immigrants. The small city thus
acted as a magnet for the neighbouring counties; the large city
attracted strangers from other parts or provinces; but only the
great capitals exercised an international influence on migration.
Moreover, not only did the big cities attract more migrants from
further afield, but more of these were from other smaller cities
that thus served as 'staging points' in the concentration process :
'The mode of internal migration . . . proceeds *staffelweise*, from
farm to village, from village to town, from town to city, from city
to metropolis'. And what of *emigration* from the cities? 'It follows the general laws already formulated. It is overwhelmingly

short-distance . . . since so much of it is directed into the suburbs.'

What of the character of the migrants? Weber found that more women migrated than men, but for shorter distances, for marriage rather than for paid employment. The migrants tended to be young adults, more than half usually in the 20–40 age range. As much as 80 per cent of the adult population of great cities was of outside birth. And two-thirds of the immigrants had lived in the great city less than 15 years.

Population Structure of the New Cities

Weber's next step was to examine the demographic structure of the new cities, for he felt that before any estimate could be made of the influence which the process of concentration exerts upon the industrial and social life of the nation, it was necessary to study closely the structure and composition of the city populations themselves. 'For after all that is said in derogation of the effects of mere association upon people's lives, it remains true that differences in the physical composition of any population do really explain many of its peculiarities.' What were notable demographic characteristics of the cities in 1899? Weber found that the cities contained a larger proportion of women, and of foreigners, than did the rest of the country, and had divorce rates three to four times those in the country. There was a regular increase in the proportion of women to men as one ascended from the smaller to the larger cities, and a parallel decrease in the married in each age group. The excess of women was among the city-born rather than the newcomers. Fewer girls than boys were born in the city compared with the country, but infant mortality was found to bear with more severity on boys rather than girls, and violent deaths affected principally men, because city occupations were more dangerous to the health of males than country occupations, as were vice, crime and excesses of other kinds which shorten life.

As for age structure, Weber said that the normal curve was thought to be a pyramid with the newly born at the base and the old at the apex. However, as disturbed by immigration to the cities, it formed a 'top-shape', bulging in the middle-age period. He said,

With more persons in the active period of life . . . one would expect city life to be easier and more animated (and) to find more energy and enterprise in cities, more radicalism, less conservatism, more vice, crime and impulsiveness generally. Birth-rates should be high in cities and death rates low, on account of age-grouping.

He also found that the death rate was lowest in rural areas and steadily increased with the size of the city, primarily a result of high infant mortality.

Clearly, the concentration of population produces an enormous drain on the vitality of people. It may be affirmed that the excessive urban mortality is due to lack of pure air, water and sunlight, together with uncleanly habits of life induced thereby. Part cause, part effect, poverty often accompanies uncleanliness : poverty, overcrowding, high rate of mortality, are usually found together in city tenements.

But this 'most difficult problem' was 'not incapable of solution' through building regulation, slum clearance, public baths.

As for the rest, education must be trusted to teach the city-poor proper sanitary habits. Education is no doubt a process both long and toilsome; but it is withal a hopeful process and forms the basis of modern democracy.

This led to Weber's final observation that

considering the effort devoted to improving the healthfulness of cities, one would naturally expect a diminution of their death rates in recent years, and such progress is evident, with larger cities leading the way.

Urbanisation and the Moral Order

Did these data mean that urbanisation necessarily brought with it degeneracy and moral decay? Weber contested the widespread view, so ably reviewed by Morton and Lucia White (1962), that city men are less healthy, vigorous and capable, both physically and mentally, than country men; that cities are the site and city life the cause of deterioration of the race. He reported, rather, that the growth of cities, like the growth of manufacturing on which it rested, favoured the development of a body of artisans and factory workmen. The city-born worked in higher status occupations than new migrants. The townsmen were more efficient industrial units than rural immigrants. The concentration of population in cities promoted the process of bringing capable men to the front. A country man coming to the city was thus seen as beginning a slow ascent up the social and economic ladder. City life produced or maintained fewer of the severer physical infirmities, like blindness, deaf-mutism, and idiocy than did the country, but it did favour the increase of insanity. The cities had a better educated population. The cities had a larger proportion of church members, but fewer church buildings, than smaller places.

On the other hand, he reported that the suicide rate was higher in urban than rural communities. 'Suicide is really one of the penalties paid for progress . . . resulting from failures in the struggle for existence.' The statistics of crime showed cities to have several times the rates of the country. And, 'as for vice, illegitimacy was far higher in the cities, prostitution was a city institution, and cities had a relatively larger number of saloons than the rural parts'.

In summation, Weber felt that the balance-sheet of urbanisation was good rather than bad : 'The fact must not be overlooked that the city affords more opportunities for the exhibition of virtues as well as of vices.' He noted that, economically, the concentration of large masses of people at once multiplies human wants and furnishes the means of their satisfaction; and the benefits are communicated to the surrounding country, which finds in the cities a market for its production and stimulus for the diversification of the same. Further, 'socially, the influence of the cities is similarly exerted in favour of liberal and progressive thought. The variety of occupations, interests, and opinions in the city produces an intellectual friction, which leads to broader and freer judgment and a great inclination to and appreciation of new thoughts, manners and ideals.' As the seat of political power, as the nursery of arts and sciences, as the centre of industry and commerce, Weber felt that the city represented the highest achievements of political, intellectual and industrial life. He also considered the rural population to be not merely conservative, but to be full of error and prejudice : 'It receives what enlightenment it possesses from the city.' The growth of cities, he felt, not only increases a nation's economic power and energy, but quickens the national pulse :

The city is the spectroscope of society; it analyses and sifts the population, separating and classifying the diverse elements. The entire progress of civilisation is a process of differentiation, and the city is the greatest differentiator.

But, he cautioned, all was not necessarily positive. If the cities differentiate, they also produce extremes. The most hopeless poverty, as well as the most splendid wealth, are found in the cities. The danger of class antagonism is particularly grave, and the complexity of city government, the multifariousness of its duties, make it the most difficult kind of government to watch. The difficulties are enhanced by the large floating population which is a necessary accompaniment of migration. Moreover, he felt that the industrial system

engenders the essentially egoistic, self-seeking and materialistic attitude . . . No one can view with equanimity the continual drift of the population to the cities where it will be subject to such demoralising influences . . . the larger the town the feebler the bonds of moral cohesion.

A BODY OF THEORY EMERGES

Adna Weber was not alone at the turn of the century in recognising that things had changed or in calling for further changes that might make things better. Frederic C. Howe (1905), alongside Lincoln Steffens, one of the most influential of Progressive writers in the United States, stated the case quite clearly :

The modern city marks an epoch in our civilisation. Through it, a new society has been created. Life in all its relations has been altered. A new civilization has been born . . . Society has developed into an organism like the human body, of which the city is the head, heart and centre of the nervous system . . . It is an organism capable of conscious and concerted action, responsive, ready and intelligent . . . contributing to the formation of definite political and social ideals.

As such hopes were being expressed, European social philosophers were busy codifying the revolutionary changes they felt industrial urbanisation had wrought. The basic questions asked were : What kind of a difference does urban living make? Why does it make this difference? The resulting theories served to guide both academic and lay thought about the city in the first half of the twentieth century, to motivate a range of social activists and planners, and to shape their plans and policies.

It was assumed axiomatically that the industrial metropolis marked a social watershed. The strategy of the European scholars who sought to codify the nature of the change was thus to develop theories of contrast. Polar distinctions were made between two types of society, traditional and modern, in the attempt to highlight the revolutionary changes that spanned the watershed.

One such distinction was drawn by Sir Henry Maine (1861). Maine saw progress as involving the gradual dissolution of family dependency and the growth of individual obligation. This involved the gradual replacement of obligations based upon status and position of the individual within the family by those based upon contract and limited liability. The change from status to contract was paralleled, he felt, in the way in which property (particularly land) is owned. Held in common by the rural kinship group, in cities land became just another exchangeable commodity, so that the individual was no longer tied to it or to the family.

Following Maine, Ferdinand Tönnies (1887) argued that two periods could be distinguished in the history of all great cultural systems. The modern state, science, cities and large-scale trade, he felt, represented the prime movers in the transition from the first to the second, thus playing their roles in an irreversible process of social evolution. The first period he called *gemeinschaft*. In it the basic unit or organisation was the family or kin-group, within which roles and responsibilities were defined by traditional authority, and social relations were instinctive and habitual. Cooperation was guided by custom. The second period Tönnies called *gesellschaft*. In it, social and economic relationships are based upon contractual obligations among individuals, whose roles become specialised. Returns to the individual are no longer based upon customary rights, but upon competitive bidding for labour, as one of several factors of production in the market place. The major groups that influence the individual are no longer kin, but professional peers. Family associations are secondary. Social relations are based upon rationality and efficiency, not tradition.

Émile Durkheim (1893) proceeded from the foundations laid by Tönnies. Durkheim saw increasing division of labour an irreversible historical-biological process involving the development of human civilisation from a segmental one to an organised one. The segmental society was based on blood relations, comprising a succession of similar all-embracing kin-groups. Modernisation involved the grouping of these little societies into larger aggregates. One result was the formation of territorial states. Another was occupational organisation of society, with individuals grouped by the nature of the social activity they perform. The increasing social division of labour was, in turn, due to increasing numbers of individuals within cities and to the multiplication of interactions and contacts.

Georg Simmel (1902) also distinguished two states of society and explored their psychological correlates. In the first he saw complete immersion of the individual in his immediate small group; in the second, the individual assumed a specialised role in mass society. In the former, the total personality of the individual was determined and dominated by the group; in the latter, individuality became protected by a condition of limited liability involving participation in different special-interest groups relating to each specialised aspect of life. Simmel, therefore, saw a fundamental contrast between rural and small town life on the one hand and the metropolis on the other. A steady rhythm of habitual behaviour existing at the unconscious level characterised the former, whereas the constant external stimulus of the latter was seen to require constant conscious response. Simmel considered that the metropolis thus sustains the individual's autonomous personality. The individual becomes more free, but there is also a threat : that impersonal precision and calculability in external relations of the individual tend to displace the personality. This is because, as the size of groups increases, so does specialisation, and so does differentiation within the metropolis.

These contrasts were restated by the American sociologist William Graham Sumner (1907). Sumner differentiated 'folkways', instinctive or unconscious ways of satisfying human needs, and 'stateways', the contractual relations mediated by state institutions. The essential contrast he saw was between unconscious traditionalism and conscious innovation. In the former, mores are imposed by society; in the latter, they are mediated by the state and experienced in cities. Almost as an echo came the remarks of Delos F. Wilcox (1907) :

The city is, indeed, the visible symbol of the annihilation of distance and the multiplication of interests . . . Among the business and professional classes, a man's most intimate associates may be scattered over the whole city, while he scarcely knows his next door neighbour's name . . . The city transforms men as if by magic and newcomers are absorbed and changed into city men.

The capstone of this line of thought came in the classics of Max Weber (1920). Weber saw the main trend in human history as that of the increased rationalisation of society. Traditional behaviour, to him, involved automatic reactions to habitual stimuli which guide behaviour, a state in which social relations are communal (*vergemeinschaftung*). On the other hand, in modern society, behaviour is dependent upon the individual, who acts with self-conscious rationality in conditions where social relations become associative (*vergesellschaftung*). In the latter conditions, contract characterises society. Individuals become oriented to rational belief in the binding validity of an obligation and rational expectation that other parties will live up to it. Means and ends thus differ, and institutions develop to mediate the resulting contractual behaviour, and provide the certainty of rules, administered by a bureaucracy.

In Table 1 we attempt to summarise the combined polar distinctions of the social philosophers and theoreticians. The 'conventional wisdom' they produced centred on the idea that there was replacement of all-encompassing primary social relationships touching on all segments of a common life experience, based upon sentiment, custom, intimate knowledge and hereditary rights, by impersonal secondary relationships based upon specialisation. One implication was the greater reliance in the new cities upon symbolic factors, 'status symbols', to designate one's identity and place in the social system. And often the secondary contacts were felt to produce indifference, normlessness and anomie. This was because the informality of social controls and the mechanical nature of social cohesion, based as they were on folkways, mores, and social institutions that had accumulated over long periods of time, were replaced by systems of control based upon law, administrative fiat, the police, and sanctions within sub-groups that even in combination were often inadequate substitutes for primary-group ties, and thus unable to prevent the emergence of social disorganisation of major dimensions.

As the change to new urban ways of life took place, families that were production, consumption, educational and affectional units, with most functions of the individual embraced by the family, were seen to be replaced by families which had become specialised secondary groups with but few functions. Accompanying this change was the shift from extended to nuclear families. At a more general level, bureaucracies were seen to emerge, for without them mass society could not function. Government,

specialization w/ less function
sub link = bureaucracy

Table 1

Polar distinctions between pre-industrial and urban-industrial society

	Pre-Industrial Society	Urban-Industrial Society
Demographic	High mortality, fertility.	Low mortality, fertility.
Behavioural	Particularistic, prescribed. Individual has multiplex roles.	Universalistic, instrumental. Individual has specialised roles.
Societal	Kin-group solidarity, extended family, ethnic cohesion. Cleavages between ethnic groups.	Atomisation. Affiliations secondary. Professional influence groups.
Economic	Non-monetary or simple monetary base. Local exchange. Little infrastructure. Craft industries. Low specialisation. *Contract exchange*	Pecuniary base. National exchange. Extensive interdependence. Factory production. Capital intensive. *voluntary contract (eg. marriage)*
Political	Non-secular authority. Prescriptive legitimacy. Interpersonal communications; traditional bases.	Secular polity. Elected government. Mass media participation. Rational bureaucracy.
Spatial (geographical)	Parochial relationships. Close ties to immediate environment. Duplication of socio-spatial groups in a cellular net.	Regional and national interdependence. Specialized roles based upon major resources and relative location within urban-spatial system.

a special form of bureaucracy, increases because modernisation creates a highly specialised and differentiated, interdependent and more vulnerable society. And finally, because in transition to a full mass society there are many frictions, social and personal disorganisation are most manifest in those parts of society undergoing the most rapid transition, particularly among migrants and immigrants, especially the second generation moving from parental to mass-society culture.

Urbanism as a Way of Life

It remained for an American sociologist, Louis Wirth, to draw these ideas together into the single most widely accepted theory of the effects of cities on social relationships, in his famous article 'Urbanism as a Way of Life' (1938). Wirth accepted the definition of the city as a point of population concentration of large size, high density, and heterogeneity of inhabitants. What he did was to *derive from* these attributes the patterns of social interaction and their consequences for organised social life that had been outlined by the earlier philosophers: impersonality, isolation, the decline of primary group membership, and the dominance of formal organisations.

For example, he felt that it was largely the greater size of the city that produced greater volumes of human interaction. With interpersonal dependence spread over more people, there would thus be less dependence upon particular individuals. Contacts would, as a result, beome impersonal, superficial and transitory—too often viewed simply as means to individual ends.

The second feature of the new city, high population density, was seen to produce frequent physical contacts, high-pace living, the functional segregation of urban sub-areas, and the segregation of people in a residential mosaic in which people with similar backgrounds and needs consciously select, unwittingly drift, or are forced by circumstances into the same section of the city. For those unable to find a secure life in some specialised role and sub-area, the likelihood of dysfunctional, deviant or pathological behaviour was seen to increase, particularly where densities were the highest.

Finally, the greater heterogeneity of the new cities was argued to produce a distinctive series of effects. Without a common background, Wirth felt that diverse peoples tended to place emphasis on visual recognition and symbolism. Such things as the place of residence, therefore, became status symbols. With no common value sets or ethical systems, money tended to become the sole measure of worth. However, economic class distinctions tended to break down, because city-dwellers belonged to a variety of groups, a further consequence of which was the growth of mass political movements and of pluralistic interest groups within the city.

Analysis of Wirth's model by Claude Fischer (1972) showed that his theory actually had two components, a sociological one based upon Durkheim, and a social-psychological one drawn from Simmel. On the structural level, size, density and heterogeneity were thought to lead sequentially to differentiation, formalisation of institutions and anomie. On the behavioural level, urbanism was thought to produce highly selective responses to the nervous stimulation and possibilities of psychological overload in the city, opportunities for great mobility, but also adaptations to urban life in the form of social isolation and deviance. The two were put together by Wirth's informal acknowledgement of the idea that in any social system, structure operates on behaviour through the mediation of cognition, and is itself an aggregation of individual behaviour.

If one accepts this basic idea, Wirth's model can be diagrammed in the manner of Fig. 1 to show how he related his basic structural variables—size, density, and heterogeneity—to individual behaviour via high degrees of nervous stimulation that demand selective responses by the individual to prevent psychological overload. Selective response to stimuli is seen as producing, in the city structure, differentiated interest groups which, in turn, produce the opportunity for individual mobility. Mobile individuals seeking self-identity in the mass society create many complex institutional devices to maintain formal integration of diverse interest-groups, but the resulting secondary relationships also breed impersonality and isolation; too much isolation, in turn, creates anomie at the societal level, alienation at the perceptual level, and resulting individual deviance. Urbanisation, in Wirth's view, led unremittingly to social malaise.

THE ROOTS OF URBAN PLANNING

This interpretation of social change from traditional little society to modern mass society was accepted as an article of faith by social scientists and social activists alike for the first half of the

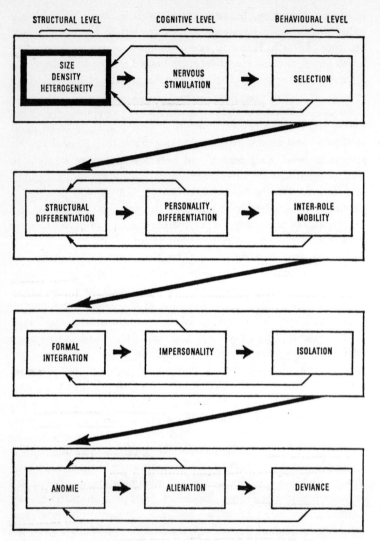

FIG. 1 Louis Wirth's theory of 'Urbanism as a Way of Life' diagrammed in causal path form

The figure is adapted from the work of Claude Fischer.

twentieth century. It moulded scientists' analyses of cities, sparked the activists' drive to change them, and produced many of the proposed solutions to urban ills advanced by a new profession, the urban planners.

The history of the American planning experience is interesting in this regard. Not only does this history provide a bridge to Chapter 2, which focuses upon the changing nature of American urbanisation in the twentieth century. It also reveals how the beliefs of the Progressive ideologists, who led the fight for social reform in America at the turn of the century, were derived from the classical ideas just discussed; how, in turn, in Progressivism are to be found many of the roots of modern American urban planning; and how American cultural values have cast this planning into particular forms.

Progressive Thought

The Progressive intellectuals—among them William Allen White, Frederic Howe, Jane Addams, Mary Parker Follett, John Dewey, Josiah Royce, Frank Giddings, Charles Horton Cooley and Robert Park—advanced their main ideas from 1890 through the First World War. It is probably incorrect to think of Progressivism as constituting a single movement. There were at least three separate threads of concern : social justice, the managed economy, and political democracy (DeWitt, 1915). At best the Progressives constituted a coalition of interests, often contradictory, involving the ambition of the new middle class to fulfil its destiny through its own bureaucratic means (Wiebe, 1967).

Yet several common features may be noted. The Progressive intellectuals idealised the small town as a place with a sense of community, with an intimacy of face-to-face personal contact and easy neighbourliness. The price paid by the individual may have been conformity, but this was felt to be bearable, even desirable. They also emphasised doing good works and the moral duty of the individual to act. A strong ethical perspective pervaded their work, orientation towards imposition of a moral order (Quandt, 1970).

What the Progressives claimed to see was the breakdown, under the impact of urbanisation and industrialisation, of the small close-knit group which they had experienced in their youth. Social organisation based on family, neighbourhood and small-town solidarity was being replaced by the more impersonal and tenuous ties

Breakdown of social ties replaced by market place ties.

Prog. view

of the market place. The division of labour, together with modern methods of communication and transportation, had created a physical unity based on the interdependence of parts—an urban, industrial order whose size and complexity precluded the traditional sense of belonging. A moral unity corresponding to this economic web had not yet emerged. Older forms of social control had been weakened; individuals in the cities had lost direct, spontaneous and intimate contacts with social reality. The restraints of public opinion and a common cause with neighbours that occurred in small towns was lacking. The city was too complex and impersonal to create a sense of identification on the part of the individual. Indeed, its bureaucratic complexities discouraged the feeling of belonging, while class conflict, complexity and physical isolation of social classes impeded mutual understanding. What was needed, the Progressives argued, was a greater psychic and moral integration to match the increasing physical integration of society. In this vision the small community became the scale model for the larger one. Its values of intimacy, mutual identification, and face-to-face communication appeared in the Progressives' blueprint for the city, the province and the nation.

Emphasising the importance of face-to-face communication, Mary Parker Follett sought to establish community centres in the public schools, agencies that would integrate local organisations and overcome civic apathy. The idea of genuine democracy led to the idea that all persons should contribute to neighbourhood purposes through direct and regular interchange. In this framework Jane Addams, America's most distinguished social worker, began her Hull House settlement in Chicago, and from that experience grew the Settlement House Movement, as well as pressures for local self-government as the antithesis of City Hall controls and corruption, such as was exemplified by Boss Tweed in New York.

At the national scale, John Dewey and Robert Park felt that through communications social progress could be produced by mutual awareness of and response to society's problems. A new community of purpose would arise and produce a new moral order through creation of justice and a cooperative social order. Park thought of unity oriented to national efficiency and the scientific solutions to crime, poverty and other social ills. All that was needed for social harmony was a common purpose and the instruments of enlightenment : the schools, the press, the motion picture,

and the social survey. Thus, the great community would material-
ise. An implied communion was a religious idea as well as the central idea of democracy.

Above all, the Progressives felt the need for good government,
a regenerated civic life, that would draw persons of culture back
and not abandon the public sphere to commercialism and corrupt
Bossism. The crux of change would have to be in politics, and most
Progressives advanced the ideal of democratic capitalism. This
ideal rested on the premise that education and communication
would create the cooperation necessary to limit conflict and make
the system work.

From the 1890s through the 1920s the Progressives' views on
industrial legislation, business regulation, and political organisation reflected their support of reforms in the United States which
regulated capitalism but stopped short of government control of
the economy. Their belief in liberal reform was combined with an
antibureaucratic bias which limited their enthusiasm for big
government and the expertise which a rationalised economy required. Sharing a suspicion of large-scale organisation, they
wanted to bring centralisation and rationalisation into harmony
with the values of the small community. The political position of
the Progressives centred on the desire to regulate capitalism without capitulating to state socialism. They favoured government
protection of workers; nonpartisan politics; regulation of trusts;
child labour laws; collective bargaining; workmen's compensation;
reform of governments through the use of commissions of experts
for social engineering and scientific management; direct democracy, including direct primaries, the referendum and initiative, to
break the power of boss and party machine; and appointment and
election of specially trained experts in government, who would
appoint experts in administration to manage the cities. Thus,
urban-industrial society, rationalised by functional organisation of
city government with professional administrators, was welcomed.
Yet remote impersonal government was deplored. Attachment to
face-to-face communication and grassroots democracy made the
Progressives cling to the small community as the *sine qua non* of a
humane social order. They tried to preserve the integrity of the
small locality because it encouraged a sense of belonging; they
tried to perpetuate the importance of local politics because it fos-
tered civic and political participation.

In these concerns of the Progressives are to be found the roots of American urban planning, which was thus a product of the first forthright attempts to confront what was perceived to be the new urban reality. Only at the end of the nineteenth century did men seriously question whether laissez-faire market-place economics would suffice in dealing with housing and the use of urban land; only then did economists become so concerned that neither monopolies nor the provision of public goods would respond to the laws of demand and supply that they were willing to countenance direct public regulation. Thus, only thereafter was there a search for the norms of public intervention designed to control land use and improve the quality of housing. A variety of threads are intertwined : landscape architecture, the City Beautiful Movement, and pressures for housing reform.

Landscape Architecture
Frederick Law Olmsted, America's first great landscape architect, and others, heirs to the romantic Gothic revival, tried to establish new criteria for urban form. Much influenced by Edward Bellamy's novel *Looking Backward* (1888), which was a nostalgic attempt to capture the imagined simplicity of an earlier, less complex, more socially responsive, American way of life, they reacted against the high densities and crowding of the city. Instead, they espoused ideas of the 'city in a garden' and they developed the prototypic American suburb, thus producing the two most distinctive urban innovations of the New World.

Adna Weber recognised the significance of what was happening, for he concluded *The Growth of Cities in the Nineteenth Century* by remarking that

the most encouraging feature of the whole situation is the tendency . . . towards the development of suburban towns. The significance of this tendency is that it denotes . . . a diminution of the *intensity* of concentration. Such a new distribution of population combines at once the open air and spaciousness of the country with the sanitary improvements, comforts and associated life of the city. . . . The rise of the suburbs it is, which furnishes the solid basis of hope that the evils of city life, so far as they result from overcrowding, may be in large part removed. If concentration of population seems desired to continue, it will be a modified concentration which offers the advantages of both city and country life.

One of the facets of this change was the attempt to bring the country into the city by developing comprehensive park-boulevard systems. But such development necessitated long-range systematic planning for parks and open space beyond the city's limits. Thus, park planning became the source of regional planning, beginning with the Boston Metropolitan Park Commission in 1890, and, following the influential Chicago Exhibition of 1893, leading to Master Plans for the City Beautiful, such as the Burnham Plan for Chicago and Chicagoan Walter Burley Griffin's 1912 plan for Australia's new capital city, Canberra. Burnham inspired generations of planners with his admonition : 'Make no little plans; they have no magic to stir men's blood', and Chicago, it might be recalled, readopted 'the city in a garden' as its civic motto when it rebuilt after the 1871 fire. Although that rebuilding involved invention of the steel-frame skyscraper and the elevator that epitomised the high densities and core-orientation of the later industrial metropolis, it was in Chicago that some of the early experimentation with the modern suburb, with its winding streets, took place, following the building of Llewellyn Park, America's first planned romantic suburb, in New Jersey by Alexander Jackson Davis. Olmsted's and Calvert Vaux's Riverside, Illinois and Brookline, Massachusetts, were planned to have picturesque informality, blending human and natural environments in ways that contrasted with the right angles, flat surfaces and straight lines of the grid-iron town.

The ramifications extended further than this, however. Ebenezer Howard, the originator of the Garden City's first experiment, Letchworth, designed it as a city in a garden. But, in many respects Howard's concept of the Garden City as an alternative to the Victorian industrial metropolis and a counter to speculative capitalism was alien to the American scene. Howard argued that a new order could be achieved only by reversing the trend of concentration by means of planned decentralisation into small, balanced cities that combined the best of rural life with the fruits of industrial occupations, in which land was regulated co-operatively rather than competitively, supported by effective public controls. On the other hand, Americans came to favour limited controls on the laissez-faire development of garden suburbs.

XI The City Beautiful Movement

In the closing years of the nineteenth century, the civic endeavours marking the beginnings of American city planning were derived from landscape architecture and were mainly aesthetic. The basic idea was that of the need for a planned unity of the entire city as a work of art, supported by a Master Plan for land use and by a comprehensive zoning ordinance to maintain the plan. New environmental ideals were advanced, as was the notion that planning was essential if the industrial city was to be saved from what was perceived to be progressive physical and moral deterioration. As one reporter remarked after attending a meeting of young architect planners in 1899: 'Beauty in high places is what we want; beauty in our municipal buildings, our parks, squares and courts.' From such notions came the idea that the role of planning was to produce the City Beautiful. Inspiration was drawn from such sources as Major Pierre Charles L'Enfant's baroque plan for Washington, D.C., and Baron Haussmann's transformation of Paris in 1853.

More than any other base, the City Beautiful Movement provided the stimulus for American city planning. It began with the Chicago Exhibition of 1893 and had its first forthright expression in the Washington plan of 1902. Following the Washington example, by 1913 43 cities had prepared similar plans—the apogee was Burnham's *Plan* for *Chicago* (1909) which followed his 1905 plans for Manila and San Francisco—and 233 cities were engaged in some civic improvement programme. Out of this activity there emerged two aspects of local planning that remain in common use today: the professional consultant, and the quasi-independent planning commission composed of leading citizens. The first commissions were created in 1907–9, and the idea spread rapidly. Over 700 commissions were created in the 1920–30 decade. Private consultants prepared one-shot Master Plans, and planning commissions administered them through the mechanism of zoning and subdivision control.

Housing Reform

As the architects and planners developed their ideas, minimal structural and sanitary standards for urban housing were, simultaneously, being sought by housing reformers. Linked with the drive for better public health was the felt need for public decision-making to control the deleterious consequences of private interests thought to be selfishly exploiting the tenement-bound working poor. Housing and building codes were thus linked to environmental controls for public health purposes. As a result, environmental standards were gradually improved. Housing standards were formulated and enforced, sanitary sewers were constructed, streets were paved, and refuse disposal was brought under control. But whereas in Britain, Germany, and Belgium, effective means of creating a low-cost housing supply were being developed—charitable trusts, for example, pioneered by investing in limited-profit, reasonable rental flats—and slum clearance and housing programmes under municipal direction had already been designed, in the United States city and state housing codes mimicked the New York State Tenement House Law of 1901. This law was based upon model codes formulated by economist Lawrence Veiller, founder of the National Housing Association, supporter of restrictive housing codes, but ardent opponent of the European 'constructive' type legislation as socialistic. Public bodies, he felt, should not replace private enterprise. The proper public role was simply to establish standards and set limits to the market-place— to regulate, rather than to substitute for market-place economics. Restrictive legislation spread, and while it provided a means of controlling new construction, it solved neither the problem of a low-income housing supply nor that of the urban slums in the United States.

Planning Professionalises

Many of the foregoing efforts involved what Leonard Reissman (1964) has called 'visionary planning for urban utopias'. Out of them emerged a new idea that grew in importance in the twentieth century, *the belief that men could consciously and effectively plan and control the physical environment of their communities to produce sought-after social consequences.* To each of the visionaries, the industrial metropolis presented a problem environment. The vision in each case involved a physical plan for building into reality those forms, social values and human qualities believed necessary for the ideal city to emerge. There was disenchantment with industrial urbanism, and a 'spatial wish'—the projection of the utopia into space—with the attendant idea that physical planning for land use and housing would produce the desired social results. Such was the basis on which urban planning professionalised.

By the end of the first decade of the twentieth century, the concepts of urban planning were widely accepted in North America. Professional city planning, devoted to conscious control of urban environments through regulatory measures, emerged after 1909, in which year was founded the National Conference of City Planning, followed by the American City Planning Institute in 1917. Thereafter, universities initiated their first training programmes for planners, public administrators, and city managers. New York introduced the first comprehensive zoning resolution in 1916, providing the planners with some control over urban land use. Cities around the country followed suit; through their mimicry, New York's innovations diffused—albeit, by lagged emulation—to 981 cities and towns by 1930.

The popularity of zoning bears closer inspection, however. Since in theory it was to be the main instrument for regulating urban development, it might be concluded that it reflected some change in Americans' laissez-faire attitudes to the urban land market. Nothing could be further from the truth. Zoning became popular precisely because it was touted as means of *protecting* property values. Single-family homes were secured from intrusions of undesirable uses, but multi-family, commercial and industrial areas were commonly overzoned. And seldom did the planning commission or the zoning board of appeals resist proposals for rezoning or variances to permit 'higher and better uses'. The planning commission in a social sense and the zoning ordinance in a real estate sense even today represent middle- and upper-class values and are conservative holding operations against the forces of social change.

To the extent that planning was concerned with parks, boulevards and civic centres, the same conservatism prevailed, for such orientations ensured that the claims of the polity did not become an issue. The achievement of those limited goals required public investment, rather than controls; the orientation was consistent with the upper middle-class constituency of plans for civic design. By nature suspicious of governmental controls, especially at the local level, this powerful interest group responded enthusiastically to objectives like beautification through public investment. At the same time, the radical alternatives of the Garden City movement were eschewed, as was active involvement in provision of low-income housing. American realtors turned Garden Cities into middle-class suburbs. American planning became essentially conservative, emphasising municipal efficiency. Businessmen turned the City Beautiful Movement into a publicly financed programme for maintaining the commercial importance of the central business district. Broad reform objectives were replaced in the planning profession, as it became institutionalised, by an increasingly narrow focus on technical skills.

Only in private groups—for example, the Regional Planning Association of America, spearheaded by Clarence Stein, Henry Wright, Frederick Ackerman, Benton MacKaye and Lewis Mumford—did there remain concern for direct housing programmes, for new towns, and for regional reconstruction of urban forms. Mumford had been much influenced by the Scottish biologist and planner Patrick Geddes. Geddes set up a settlement house in Edinburgh in 1887 three years after Samuel A. Barnett established Toynbee Hall, the first such experiment, in London, and two years before Jane Addams founded Hull House in Chicago in 1889. He was well aware of Charles Booth's analyses of social problems in London and of the Fabian socialists' calls for reform, and, as a contemporary of Ebenezer Howard, gave his support to the Garden City movement. Geddes influenced several generations of students, including Sir Patrick Abercrombie, who subsequently developed the Greater London Plan. He helped stimulate the first town planning legislation in Britain in 1909. He proposed urban renewal, neighbourhood rehabilitation, community action and participatory democracy. And he invented the term *conurbation* to describe constellations of cities sprawling together. Like Geddes, Mumford argued that public controls over urban form and land use were not enough, that amelioration of the environmental and social pathologies of existing cities was impossible without fundamental changes in residential design, housing finance, and urban-regional planning.

It was in Britain rather than in the United States that these ideas took root, however, as we shall see in Chapter 4. Before the First World War, the London County Council had embarked upon programmes of slum clearance and provision of low-income housing, and by the mid 1930s local authority housing and other state-aided construction was already accounting for half of all new housing in Britain. By the late 1930s a major policy aim had emerged : to provide satisfactory housing for all at rents within their capacity to pay. Along with this came a concern lest the private housing sector promote 'unhealthy' urban sprawl not conducive to full community development. There was the first Town Planning Act of 1909, the Town Planning Institute in 1914, the International Garden Cities Federation in 1913, and then, with F. J. Osborn and C. B. Purdom leading the movement, came the construction of Welwyn Garden City. Even more influential action followed in the 1930s. Finally, as the Town and Country Planning Association (1941), the Garden City activists had their major impact on Britain's post-war reconstruction policies, and indeed, on post-Second World War urban development policies throughout Western Europe, for their plans were extensively copied elsewhere, for example in Sweden. The plans were clear : large urban centres should be decentralised through the planned development of small satellite cities; growth should be controlled through restrictive land use and building licensing policies; the 'unhealthy' growth of the largest cities, in particular, should be stopped; urban 'sprawl' should be halted by girdling green belts; the public should provide an effective counterpoint to speculative private development.

In the American city, on the other hand, a tradition of 'privatism' prevailed. This tradition has been called by Sam Bass Warner Jr (1968)

the most important element of American culture for understanding the development of cities. [It] has meant that the cities of the United States depended for their wages, employment, and general prosperity upon the aggregate successes and failures of thousands of individual enterprises, not upon community action. It has also meant that the physical forms of American cities, their lots, houses, factories and streets have been the outcome of a real estate market of profit-seeking builders, land speculators, and large investors. [And it] has meant that the local politics of American cities have depended for their actors, and for a good deal of their subject matter, on the changing focus of men's private economic activities.

Privatism has persisted throughout America's urban history. The realisation that this is so is essential to an understanding of American urban dynamics in the twentieth century, to which we turn in Chapter 2.

2 Twentieth-Century Urbanisation: The North American Experience

By the end of the First World War, interpretations of the industrial metropolis had been provided, its ills had been diagnosed, new social movements had emerged, and city planning had professionalised. During the two inter-war decades most American social scientists simply accepted the conventional wisdom of the social theorists as they analysed cities. Hope Tisdale, for example, summarised what had by then become a generally accepted definition in her paper 'The Process of Urbanisation' (1942). Louis Wirth, likewise, was responsible for the definitive codification of the social theory in 'Urbanism as a Way of Life'. But even as Tisdale and Wirth wrote, American cities were being transformed. It is to the nature of this transformation that we now should turn, because it created a new and different process of urbanisation and a contrasting array of human consequences.

CONSEQUENCES OF METROPOLITAN CONCENTRATION

'Urbanisation', Tisdale wrote in the manner of Adna Weber,

is a process of population concentration. It proceeds in two ways : the multiplication of the points of concentration and the increasing in size of individual concentrations. . . . Just as long as cities grow in size or multiply in number, urbanisation is taking place. . . . Urbanisation is a process of becoming. It implies a movement . . . from a state of less concentration to a state of more concentration.

The statistics of the twentieth century apparently bear out Tisdale's contention. Care is, of course, required in defining the areas for which the data on concentration are reported. As the U.S. Bureau of the Census noted early in the century :

. . . the population of the corporate city frequently gives a very inadequate idea of the population massed in and around that city, constituting the greater city. . . . [The boundaries of] large cities in few cases . . . limit the urban population which that city repre-

sents or of which it is the centre ... If we are to have a correct picture of the massing or concentration of population in extensive
urban areas ... it is necessary to establish *metropolitan districts*
which will show the magnitude of each of the principal population centres.

Spelling out the idea further, in 1960 the Bureau of the Budget's
Committee on Metropolitan Area Definition wrote :

The general concept of a metropolitan area is one of an integrated
economic and social unit with a recognised large population
nucleus. ... The Standard Metropolitan Statistical Area will include a central city, and adjacent counties that are found to be
metropolitan in character and economically and socially integrated with the county of the central city.

The percentage of the American population living in such metropolitan areas increased progressively during the twentieth century.
At the beginning of the century, 60 per cent of the population
lived on farms and in villages. By 1970, 69 per cent of the population resided in metropolitan areas. Clearly, metropolitan concentration was the dominant feature of population redistribution during the first half of the century. But as the century progressed, the
patterns of population redistribution *within* these metropolitan
areas became of increasing importance.

*'Our Cities', 1937: National Concern with Urban Problems
    Emerges*

Many of the consequences of this rapid burst of metropolitan concentration came to the forefront of public attention in the 1930s,
as the crash of 1929 was followed by America's first venture into
social policy, the New Deal. Faced by massive urban unemployment, among the creations of this period was the National Resources Committee, charged with recommending ameliorative
action. One of its subcommittees prepared a report entitled *Our
Cities: Their Role in the National Economy* (1937), and concluded in a vein that has been repeated in public inquiries ever
since (for few of the problems have been solved) :

1. The most drastic inequalities of income and wealth are found
within the urban community....
2. ... localities, by means of subsidies, tax exemptions, and free
sites, have indiscriminately attracted enterprises which did not
mesh with the rest of the community's industries and which sooner
or later helped to throw the entire industrial pattern out of
gear....

3. Rapid obsolescence of physical plan and plant is another problem. . . .

4. Competing forms of transportation have left their disrupting imprint on the national urban pattern. . . .

5. The unparalleled growth of cities has been accompanied by uncontrolled subdivision and speculative practices. . . . We are now faced with the problem of arriving at a rational urban land policy. . . .

6. Urban housing is one of the most burdensome problems. . . .

7. Urban public health is endangered particularly in blighted areas and among low income groups. . . .

8. The city with its diversity of ethnic, religious, and cultural strains is the haven par excellence of many widely varying types of personalities . . . but in this heterogeneity the city also finds some of its weightiest problems . . . the urban way of life is often socially disconnected though economically interdependent. Allegiances may become group, class, or sectional.

9. . . . city youths . . . are still barred from higher educational opportunities they might well utilize. . . .

10. Juvenile delinquency, organised crime, and commercial rackets are among the vexations of the city. . . .

11. Urban public finance is another emerging problem of vast proportions. . . .

12. Another of the city's tasks is the adjustment of the traditional scope of urban powers. . . .

13. Our overlapping medley of independent governmental units was . . . never intended for the sprawling metropolitan regions of America. . . .

14. . . . we are still faced in some cities with systematic evasions of civil service laws, irresponsible political leadership, and official tolerance of discriminatory or questionable administrative practices. . . .

The Committee concluded that :

All in all there has been more widespread national neglect of our cities than of any other major segment of our national existence. . . . (But) the delayed proddings of conscience and the urge for mass consumption of commodities and services unite to thrust us forward towards sounder national policies . . . (that) would accomplish the following :

1. Improvement of the standards of urban life and raising of the level of living conditions. . . .

2. Elimination of urban blight and erosion; and, above all, abolition of the slum. . . .

3. Better knowledge about the conditions of the cities. . . .

4. Better planned industrial location. . . .

5. National-urban preparedness to meet insecurity and unem-

ployment . . . our Committee does not anticipate the decline of urban population or the wholesale dispersion of great centres of population . . . the realistic answer to the question of a desirable urban environment lies not in wholesale dispersion, but in the judicious reshaping of the urban community and region by systematic development and redevelopment in accordance with forward looking and intelligent plans.

Systematic concern for the cities was thus focused on housing, slum clearance, and urban renewal. The Federal Housing Administration had been established to stimulate construction and home ownership through insuring mortgages under certain circumstances. The Housing Act of 1937 created the United States Housing Authority and introduced slum clearance to the American scene, to produce employment and help in 'priming the pump' of the economy, to eliminate the worst housing and to provide public housing for the poor. At the same time the Works Progress Administration provided the money to employ planners to conduct a greater volume of urban studies than had ever been undertaken before. The efficacy and orientation of these efforts is a point to which we shall return later on in this chapter, because by their very nature they conformed to the dominance of privatism in American society.

Wirth Evaluated
It was Louis Wirth who, as a memer of the Urbanism Committee, provided the theoretical basis for the committee's finding that urbanisation had produced the long list of ills. His theory was accepted by an entire generation of social scientists and urban policymakers as the new flood of urban research ran its course. Like Wirth, most researchers firmly believed that the essential nature of the city—population size, density and heterogeneity—produced a series of psychological and social consequences in two mutually reinforcing ways. On the individual level, urban life was felt to expose the resident to a constant bombardment of stimuli : sights, sounds, people, social demands for attention, concern and action. Under this overstimulation, coping mechanisms to defend the organism isolated men from their environment and from other people. The urbanite, therefore, became aloof from others, superficial in his contacts with them, blasé, sophisticated and indifferent to the events occurring about him. His relationships to others

became restricted to specific roles and tasks in a business-like way, and he thus was thought to be estranged from his fellow man.

On the aggregate level, concentration, it was believed, in conjunction with the economic principles of competition and comparative advantage, led to differentiation and diversification. The larger the community, the more divided and specialised the labour, the greater the number and variety of social groups and the greater the differences among neighbourhoods. To hold such a splintered society together different social mechanisms were seen to be needed : means of formal integration such as written laws, impersonal rules of etiquette, and special agencies of social control, education, communication and welfare. Formal institutions were, however, believed to be inadequate to avoid a state of anomie—that condition of society in which social bonds between individuals and their groups are weak, as are the rules of proper and permissible behaviour. Such a state of anomie was argued to result in social and personality disorganisation, deviance and, once again, individual isolation.

How accurate has Wirth's model been as a guide to understanding the consequences of twentieth-century American urbanisation? Proceeding in sequence through Fig. 1 let us review more recent evidence that bears on the validity of Wirth's postulates, drawing on the work of Fischer (1972b). Wirth began by defining the city as a 'relatively large, dense and permanent settlement of socially heterogeneous individuals', growing rapidly through immigration, and he hypothesised that *urbanism causes certain social phenomena.*

This beginning had some validity. As size, density and heterogeneity increase, residents of cities are indeed recipients of exponentially increasing amounts and diversity of sensory stimuli (inputs) demanding conscious responses (outputs), both physical and social. The recipients, consequentially, face problems of coping with such high stimulation, and there is real danger of information overload, producing stress, strain, tension and ultimately, such behavioural manifestations as psychiatric disorders. Staney Milgram (1970) has suggested that there is ample evidence of the high information inputs, and coping techniques that include such protective adaptations as blocking off inputs, giving less time to each input, and selectively filtering them to reduce intensity— in Wirth's terms 'isolation', 'transitoriness', 'superficiality' and 'secondary relationships'. But as Leo Srole (1972) has shown, recent evidence no longer supports the proposition that mental disorder frequencies are greater in cities.

Counter point

As total stimulation increases, the range to which each person responds has been shown to narrow. On the societal level such narrowing produces specialisation and structural differentiation. One well-documented result is an increasing number of social roles and institutions; another is the division of labour; and others include the separation of work and home, geographic differentiation of the city into distinct land-use zones, and the emergence of segregated, homogeneous residential neighbourhoods. This structural differentiation is reproduced, according to Wirth's theory, in the differentiation of individual personality, divided among compartmentalised roles, associations and interests, producing different identities insulated from one another by the segregation of time and situation. In turn, the theory continues, urban individuals should tend to move through more roles more rapidly and more often than others, both in daily, weekly and other cycles, and secularly via the life cycle and social mobility. The evidence on such mobility is mixed, however; mobility among urbanites is not consistently higher than in rural areas, and neither is the degree of structural differentiation.

To continue with Wirth, as structural differentiation and role transiency increase in a system, new structures and functions were hypothesised to arise to integrate both individuals and institutions. Such formal integration involves both rational and legal procedures for governing institutional processes and interpersonal interaction. The procedures are bureaucratic, involving the functional, contractual relations that maintain order. Consistent with this analysis, Wirth hypothesised the decline of kinship, neighbourhood and informal groupings and in their place the growth of formal agencies of affiliation and control : associations, corporate enterprises, codified and mediated methods of social control and mass media.

Counter

As we shall see later, however, many studies have rejected the kinship hypothesis; strong kin group relations are maintained in cities. What seemed to be forgotten in Wirth's analysis is what has been amply demonstrated by later studies : that people actually lead their lives in much smaller milieus—their immediate families, friends and co-workers, immediate neighbourhoods and carefully selected communities. These are the groups which influence and, to a great extent, circumscribe the individual's experience. Relatively few persons, mostly those at the upper rungs of the social ladder, have in any sense large parts of cities as their meaningful social environments. Thus, the metropolitan experience is largely an experience mediated by the individual's immediate interaction networks within one portion of a city. The most immediate personal context is the family. It is true that the traditional family structure appears less frequently in larger cities, but the social force of kinship is affected in very particular ways : the geographic dispersal of relatives and the reduction of the degree to which the family is called upon to provide aid and other services are the most apparent. However, contact with kin is no less frequent. Nor is there evidence that the social psychological importance of kin is any less in urban places. The family is a more specialised institution in cities. Whether this strengthens or weakens the family is debatable.

Accompanying formal integration, Wirth saw a cognitive complement, impersonality—the well-documented understanding of the world in terms of the formal roles and rules of interaction. Here the evidence is mixed. Herbert Gans has suggested other patterns among his ethnic 'urban villagers', and similar findings have been produced for other urban sub-groups. There is little evidence that friendships are fewer or more shallow in cities. Neither is it apparent that the cohesiveness of ethnic subcultures is reduced, or that urbanites are necessarily anonymous to their neighbours.

If the formal society environment is marked by impersonality, Wirth argued, urban individuals would be isolated from each other. The members of the 'lonely crowd' should stay aloof from each other, anonymous by minimising interactions. But many studies have rejected this notion of interpersonal estrangement, showing high levels of kin and friendship interaction and low levels of expressed sense of isolation. If rootless and isolated, Wirth continued, individuals would be less subject to group pressures, leading to a societal condition of low normative cohesion, or anomie. But again, this description of anomie has been rejected for industrial cities, and this link in Wirth's model is also a doubtful one.

In an anomic society, incongruencies exist between the understandings and motivations that individuals display and those they should have in the normative terms of the modal or 'mainstream' patterns and functional needs of the system. This lack of fit due to anomie is alienation, and it involves powerlessness (a low sense of control over one's life), normlessness (ineffectiveness of socially approved means of achieving ends), and meaninglessness (a low sense of comprehension of the events surrounding the individual). Cohesive systems adequately socialise, the theory continues, thereby producing a sense of efficacy in role-performance and adherence to the norms of the roles and complementary expectations about the results of role behaviour. The anomic city, on the other hand, results in personality-structure incongruencies. The data in this case are inconsistent and generally unsupportive. As we shall see later, alienation appears better explained by higher aspirations, lower satisfactions and a general sense of relative deprivation among certain groups of urbanites.

The final link in Wirth's theory was that between weak normative cohesion and poor personality-structure integration and deviancy in the city. Deviance in the broadest sense is behaviour that is different than that which is normatively expected—illegal, 'odd', or innovative. Each of these deviant forms reaches its maximum in large cities—innovativeness, moral deviance (alcoholism, divorce, illegitimacy), and criminality, as well as lower degrees of religious participation and greater tendencies to radicalism in politics. But again, whether Wirth's model is the appropriate one to use is seriously open to question.

Particularly questionable is the conclusion of Wirth's model that high population densities in large cities should produce a range of pathologies. An entire research stream dealing with the implications of high levels of density for human populations has gone back to Wirth's model for conceptual foundations. It may thus be worth while to explore in some detail whether this final conclusion has any validity either.

Apparent support for Wirth came from studies of laboratory rats. High densities produced increased mortality, lower fertility, neglect, aggressive conflict-oriented behaviour, withdrawal syndromes and sexual aberrations. Other animal studies have tended to support these conclusions.

However, in studies of human populations the evidence is less clear, especially when gross density is broken into such components as the number of persons per room, the number of housing units per structure, and the number of residential structures per acre, and when such factors as social class and ethnicity are taken into account. In the most careful and comprehensive investigations completed to date, Omer R. Galle (1972) thus concluded that density variables tend to simply interpret a more basic relation between social structural variables and pathologies, rather than playing a direct causative role in pathology. Further, he found the most significant elements of density affecting pathologies involving mortality, fertility, dependency, delinquency and mental illness to be persons per room and rooms per housing unit (i.e. overcrowding) rather than persons per unit area (density).

He interpreted the results as meaning that as the number of persons in a dwelling increases, so will the number of social obligations, as well as the need to inhibit individual desires. This escalation of both social demands and the need to inhibit desires becomes particularly problematic when people are crowded together in a dwelling with a high ratio of persons per room. Further, he said, crowding brings with it a marked increase in stimuli that are difficult to ignore. Third, if human beings, like many animals, have a need for territory or privacy, then overcrowding may, in fact, conflict with a basic (biological?) characteristic of man.

It then seems reasonable to expect that people would react to the incessant demands, stimulation, and lack of privacy resulting from overcrowding with irritability, weariness, and withdrawal. Furthermore, people are likely to be so completely involved in reacting to their environment that it becomes extremely difficult for them to step back, look at themselves, and plan ahead. It would certainly seem that in an overcrowded situation it would be difficult for them to follow through on their plans. Thus it might be expected that the behaviour of human beings in an overcrowded environment is primarily a response to their immediate situation and reflects relatively little regard for the long-range consequences of their acts. Such immediate environments clearly need not be urban. Indeed, the best overall conclusion one may reach is that Wirth's model is inadequate in a variety of important respects.

THE NEW TWENTIETH-CENTURY URBAN REGION

Wirth's theory may have been appropriate to the nineteenth-century industrial urbanisation from whose social theorists he derived his intellectual stimulus. The problem is that it was, even when it was formulated, a woefully inadequate guide to the twentieth-century city. The nature of urbanisation had changed and was changing as Wirth wrote. The nineteenth-century world of escalating technologies and integrating national economies created the industrial city within the nation-state. It was this new city, the industrial city as it had matured in the nineteenth and early twentieth centuries in the Western world, that became the object of Wirth's essay. Wirth believed that he offered a theory upon which to build future research. In actuality, his theory was a peroration on a city that had passed.

The concentrated industrial metropolis developed because proximity meant lower transportation and communication costs for those interdependent specialists who had to interact with each other frequently or intensively. But shortened distances meant higher densities and costs of congestion, high rent, loss of privacy, and the like. Virtually all the technological developments of more recent times have had the effect of reducing the constraints of geographic space and the costs of concentration. Modern transportation and communications have made it possible for each generation to live farther apart and for information users to rely upon information sources that are spatially distant. Decentralisation and declining overall densities have moved to the fore as dominant spatial processes. Fig. 2, for example, shows that the more recent the growth of the city, the lower its population densities in both the United States and Canada, for the later the growth of the city, the greater its dependence upon the newer technologies of the automobile, motor truck, and modern communications. Moreover, whatever the age of the city, its density has declined significantly in recent decades as even the oldest cities have responded to changing technology and increasing affluence.

Even in 1900, Adna Weber's contemporaries believed that things would change in this direction. They looked to the suburbs as a panacea for the urban ills that they attributed to congestion and high densities. H. G. Wells, for example, wrote (1902) that

many of [the] railway-begotten 'giant cities' will reach their maximum in the coming century [and] in all probability they . . . are destined to such a process of dissection and diffusion as to amount almost to obliteration . . . within a measurable further space of years. [T]*hese coming cities will not be, in the old sense, cities at*

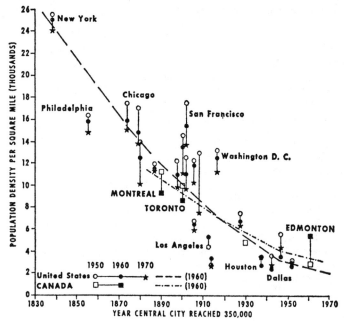

FIG. 2   The relationship between the age of large cities in North America and their changing population densities in the years 1950–70.

all; they will present a new and entirely different phase of human distribution. [italics added] [T]he social history of the middle and latter third of the nineteenth century . . . all over the civilised world is the history of a gigantic rush of population into the magic radius of—for most people—four miles, to suffer there physical and moral disaster less acute but, finally, far more appalling than any famine or pestilence that ever swept the world. . . . But . . . these great cities are no permanent maëlstroms. [N]ew forces, at present so potently centripetal in their influence, bring with them, nevertheless, the distinct promise of a centrifugal application that may finally be equal to the complete reduction of all our present congestions. The limit of the pre-railway city was the limit of man and horse. But already that limit has been exceeded, and each day brings us nearer to the time when it will be thrust outward in every direction with an effect of enormous relief. So far the only additions to the foot and horse . . . are the suburban railways. . . . The star-shaped contour of the modern great city, thrusting out . . . knotted arms of which every knot marks a station, testify . . . to the relief of pressure thus afforded. Great towns before this century presented rounded contours and grew as puff-ball swells; the modern Great City looks like something that has burst an intolerable envelope and splashed . . . the mere first rough expedient of far more convenient and rapid developments.

We are . . . in the early phase of a great development of centrifugal possibilities. . . . [A] city of pedestrians is inexorably limited by a radius of about four miles . . . a horse-using city may grow out to seven or eight. . . . [I]s it too much . . . to expect that the available area for even the common daily toilers of the great city of year 2000 . . . will have a radius of over one hundred miles?

What will be the forces acting upon the prosperous household . . . ? [T]he passion for nature . . . the allied charm of cultivation . . . [and] that craving . . . for a little private *imperium* [are] the chief centrifugal inducements.

[T]he city will diffuse itself until it has taken up considerable areas and many of the characteristics of what is now country. . . . [T]he country will take itself many of the qualities of the city. The old antithesis will . . . cease, the boundary lines will altogether disappear.

'[T]own' and 'city' will be, in truth, terms as obsolete as 'mail coach'. . . . We may call . . . these coming town provinces 'urban regions'.

Growth of Daily Urban Systems

Achieved at a pace more rapid than he anticipated, Wells' forecasts captured the essential features of the urban geography of the United States in 1970. 'City', the continuously built-up 'urbanised area', and the larger census-defined metropolis had *all* been superseded in the realities of daily life by urban regions of a new and larger scale which we can call for want of another name, 'Daily Urban Systems'.

This urban explosion can be seen in Figs. 3–6, which show the region around Detroit, Michigan, the home of the automobile which was largely responsible for the beginning of the transformation. The shades on the maps have been selected to show how previously agricultural areas were transformed to non-agricultural uses by twentieth-century urbanisation. The final map in the series also shows the outer radius of daily commuting to the city of Detroit in 1960, to give a sense of the scale of the daily ebb and flow responsible for the cohesion of the system. Fig. 7 shows the extent of the Daily Urban Systems in the United States in 1960. More than 90 per cent of the national population lived within these systems in that year.

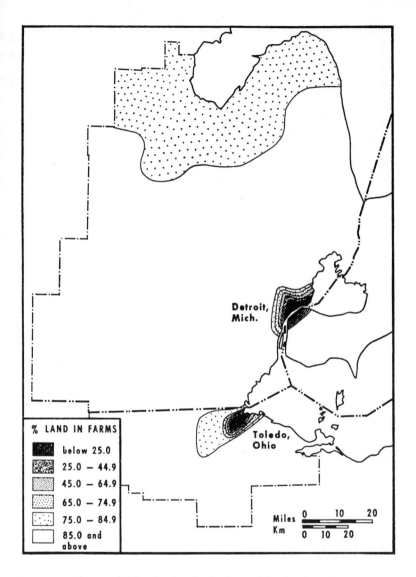

% LAND IN FARMS

■	below 25.0
▨	25.0 – 44.9
░	45.0 – 64.9
⦂	65.0 – 74.9
∴	75.0 – 84.9
□	85.0 and above

Detroit, Mich.

Toledo, Ohio

FIG. 3   Urbanisation in the Detroit region in 1900

The figure, along with the three following it, uses per cent of land in farms as an index of the extent to which non-agricultural uses have spread, and is adapted from one originally prepared by C. A. Doxiadis in his work for the Detroit Edison Company.

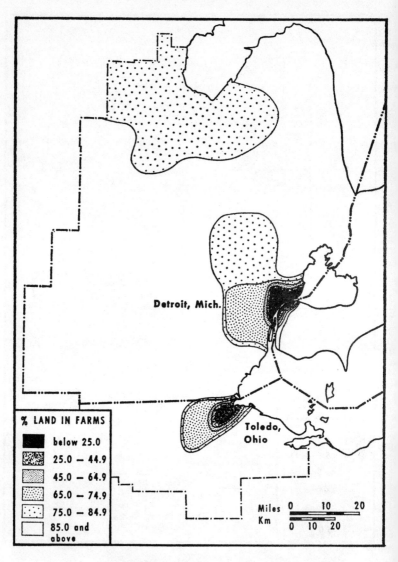

% LAND IN FARMS
- ■ below 25.0
- ▨ 25.0 — 44.9
- ▦ 45.0 — 64.9
- ▩ 65.0 — 74.9
- ∴ 75.0 — 84.9
- □ 85.0 and above

Detroit, Mich.

Toledo, Ohio

Miles 0   10   20
Km   0   10   20

FIG. 4   Urbanisation in the Detroit region in 1920

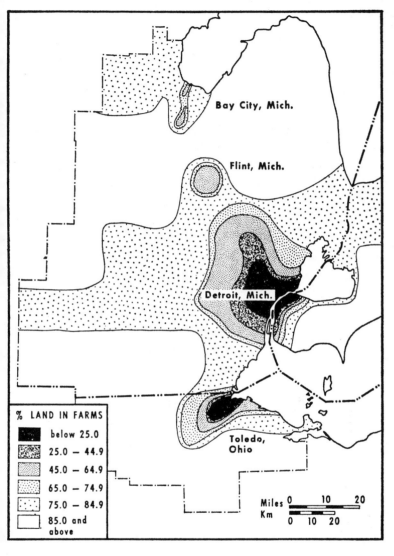

% LAND IN FARMS

- below 25.0
- 25.0 — 44.9
- 45.0 — 64.9
- 65.0 — 74.9
- 75.0 — 84.9
- 85.0 and above

Bay City, Mich.

Flint, Mich.

Detroit, Mich.

Toledo, Ohio

Miles 0   10   20
Km   0   10   20

FIG. 5   Urbanisation in the Detroit region in 1940

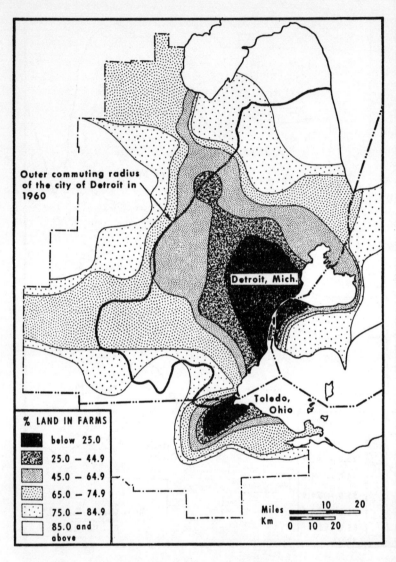

% LAND IN FARMS

■	below 25.0
▨	25.0 — 44.9
▧	45.0 — 64.9
⠿	65.0 — 74.9
⠂	75.0 — 84.9
□	85.0 and above

Outer commuting radius of the city of Detroit in 1960

Detroit, Mich.

Toledo, Ohio

Miles 10 20
Km   0 10 20

Fɪɢ. 6   Urbanisation in the Detroit region in 1959

This map also shows the outermost limits of daily commuting to the city of Detroit in 1960.

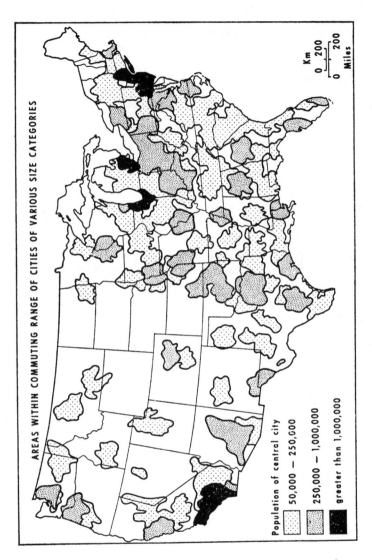

FIG. 7   Commuting areas of central cities in the United States in
1960

This map was originally prepared as part of a project in which I
re-evaluated the metropolitan area concept for the U.S. Bureau
of the Budget.

As such urban systems developed they imprinted distinctive spatial patterns on the nation. Initially these patterns were core-oriented and conical in form. To quote Raymond Vernon and Edgar Hoover's description of New York (1959):

If we think of the region as a huge conical structure in which altitude represents the concentration of human activity, we find Newark, Jersey City, Paterson, Elizabeth, Yonkers, and Bridge-port—each with a population of over 100,000—protruding as lesser peaks from its sloping flanks. Yet by any measure one cares to devise, the apex of the whole structure is on the island of Manhattan.

The growth and spread of similar cones around each city brought to the nation orderly rhythms of opportunity and welfare : as 'altitude' fell, so did population densities and economic opportunity, income and educational levels, while the poverty population grew. The American people were not ignorant of these rhythms. As Table 2 shows, the rewards to migration were substantial. They responded by emigrating from the low-income peripheries, where population then declined.

Table 2

Annual earnings gains (U.S. $) of migrants from rural south to urban north compared with rural south non-migrants of same education, race and sex

		TO SMALL NORTHERN CITIES*		TO VERY LARGE NORTHERN CITIES†	
Years after Moving		*Elementary Education*	*College Education*	*Elementary Education*	*College Education*
White Males	0–5	—	$3075	$ 600	$3075
	6–35	$1550	2175	2700	3700
Black Males	0–5	800	3875	1400	3875
	6–35	1550	2175	2000	3000

* Under 50,000 people.   † Over 750,000 people.

SOURCE: Richard Wertheimer II, *The Monetary Rewards of Migration Within the U.S.* (Washington, D.C., The Urban Institute, 1971). Reported in *Search*, vol. 1, no. 1 (January–February, 1971), p. 7.

The result by 1960 has been described very effectively by two American planners, J. Friedmann and J. Miller (1965), who said that it was possible in that year

... to interpret the spatial structure of the United States in ways that ... emphasise a pattern consisting of *one*, metropolitan areas and *two*, the inter-metropolitan periphery. Except for thinly populated parts of the American interior, the inter-metropolitan periphery includes all the areas that intervene among metropolitan regions; like a devil's mirror, much of the periphery has developed a socio-economic profile that perversely reflects the very opposite of metropolitan virility.

However, what was initially core-oriented and conical in form has itself undergone transformation. The cones of metropolitan influence had a particular shape : densities of all kinds dropped off with increasing distance at an exponential rate. This rate of drop-off is called the density gradient. An American economist, Edwin Mills (1972) has computed such density gradients for population and a variety of economic activities for a sample of American cities for the years 1910–70. The results are graphed in Fig. 8. What this graph shows is that the density gradients have

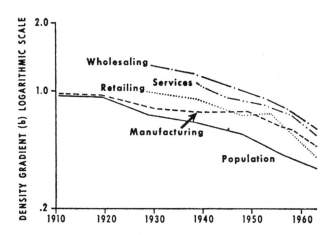

FIG. 8   Changes in the density gradients of U.S. cities in the twentieth century

The figure is plotted from data in a table prepared by Mills (1972).

TRENDS

fallen progressively over the years, meaning declining densities at the city centre, rapid outward expansion of metropolitan areas, and progressively more uniform densities across urban regions.

If the graph is examined closely, it will be seen that the pace of decentralisation appears to be accelerating. Reflecting on such acceleration, Oscar Handlin, a historian, said in 1963, apparently confirming Wells' forecasts :

The differences between city and country have been attenuated almost to the vanishing point. The movement of people, goods and messages has become so rapid and has extended over such a long period as to create a new situation. To put it bluntly, the urbanisation of the whole society may be in process of destroying the distinctive role of the modern city.

Handlin also pointed to the emergence of a new social process as the cause of the increase in the rate of change :

What is new is the effective motivation—the insistence upon constructing small, coherent communities . . . Increasingly, the men who now people the metropolis long for the security of isolation from the life about them. They strive to locate their families in space, with a minimum of connections to the hazards of the external world.

The facts of the further transformation became unmistakable in the United States in the 1960s. First, Jean Gottmann described the continuous urbanisation of the north-eastern seaboard in terms of a new geographical scale, dubbed *megalopolis*. More recently have come the findings reported by the Commission on Population Growth and the American Future (1972) about the changing nature of metropolitan growth in the United States. They show that in the 1960–70 decade the population of metropolitan areas grew by 26 millions, two-thirds from growth within constant boundaries, and one-third by annexation of expanding peripheries into which the population is now dispersing. Of the growth inside 1960 boundaries, three-quarters was due to natural increase, and of the one-quarter due to immigration, more came from overseas than from rural areas. The migration rate for farm population has been relatively constant since 1940. During this 30-year time span, the rate of out-migration has varied from 5·2 to 5·8 per cent per five-year period. The actual number of farm migrants has declined sharply, however, because of the declining numbers of farm residents. Between 1945 and 1950 the net out-migration from the farm was 1,600,000 while between 1965 and 1970 the number was 582,000. Only 5 per cent of the nation's population—less than 10 million people—was left on the farm in 1970.

The result is that *growth in the United States is now largely*

*self-generated metropolitan growth; the concentrative migration
process resulting from industrial urbanisation has ended.* Migration takes place between metropolitan areas on an inter-regional
scale, and intra-regionally through an accelerating dispersion of
people and jobs outward into the peripheries of the daily urban
systems beyond metropolitan boundaries. Table 3 shows, for example, the net migration rates of counties adjacent to metropolitan areas of different size categories between 1960 and 1970.

Table 3

*Net migration of counties adjacent to metropolitan areas
of different size categories*

Size Category	Per Cent Net Migration
5 million and over	9·7
2–5 million	3·0
1–2 million	4·4
500,000–1 million	−2·1
250–500,000	−2·8
100–250,000	−4·0
50–100,000	−6·8

SOURCE: Robert L. McNamara, 'Population Change and Net Migration
in the North Central States, 1960–70'. Report of a co-operative project,
North Central Regional Project: Population Changes in the North Central States (NC-97). To be published by the Missouri Agricultural
Experiment Station.

The new scale of urbanisation also involves increasing population mobility. The number of migrants crossing county lines in
the five-year period of 1955–60 was 50 per cent higher than in
1935–40. Nearly 40 million Americans now change their homes
each year. Roughly one in 15 Americans—a total of 13 million
people—migrate across a county line. At least a fifth of all Americans move one or more times a year, and the pace of movement
is still increasing (Packard, 1972).

When asked about where they prefer to live, Americans usually
answer that it is in suburbs and in smaller towns, in more pleasant
and less dense environments. Their pursuit of such living conditions is revealed both in the changes in densities depicted in Fig. 2
and in the recent census data. In the two decades 1950–70 the
average population density of all urbanised areas in the United

States dropped from 5408 persons per square mile to 3376; for central cities the decline was from 7786 to 4463. The central cities that grew in the wave of industrial urbanism are now experiencing declining populations. Declining central cities lost more people in the decade than were lost due to migration by declining rural counties. The list includes Baltimore, Boston, Philadelphia, Pittsburgh, Chicago, Detroit and St Louis; 15 of the 21 central cities with a population exceeding one-half million in 1960 lost population in the 1960–70 decade. Almost all metropolitan growth was, as a result, concentrated in the decade in rapidly dispersing suburban territory.

Of course, the centrifugal movement of urban population has a history that extends back into the nineteenth century. Density declines and absolute losses in the innermost zones began shortly after 1850 in New York and other large cities and became apparent in many smaller ones before that century closed. The factors underlying the centrifugal drift initially were improvements in local transportation and communication facilities and the continued expansion of the business core. Population retreated as the approach of business and industrial uses blighted the land for residential occupance and drove land values above what low intensity residential uses could sustain. A significant shift has occurred in the centrifugal trend, however. Whereas until 1950 or thereabouts there were usually high intensity uses available to bid for residential properties adjoining industrial and commercial districts, that kind of replacement has diminished and has ceased entirely in some metropolitan centres. In only five years, from 1958–63, for example, the central cities of metropolitan areas with populations exceeding 250,000 lost manufacturing jobs while 433,000 jobs were added to their suburbs. Only in a dozen major cities was there a significant expansion of new headquarters, finance and real-estate, and governmental office-space in downtown skyscrapers. Elsewhere, the continuing centrifugal movement of urban population and urban institutions is leaving a widening core of obsolescent, deteriorated and abandoned buildings where once stood the richest sources of municipal revenues.

Reasons for the Changes

Increasing scale, increasing mobility and declining density are all features of the contemporary American urban scene. Among the reasons they have become the salient characteristics of urbanisation today are the emergence of a truly national society, the rise of a post-industrial economy, the increasing connection between social and spatial mobility, the exceptional performance of the housing industry, and progressive time–space convergence resulting from substitution of improved communications for face-to-face interaction. Let us look at each of these before we turn to the human consequences of this new urbanisation, and to the ways in which American public intervention has conformed to and supported these powerful social, economic and technological forces, rather than trying to combat them.

The United States has moved progressively from merely being a political entity, comprising diverse regions held together by a common symbolism, to a true 'national' society in which changes taking place in one section of the society have an immediate and repercussive effect in all others. The change is due in large measure to the revolution in communication and transportation—the rise of national network television, coast-to-coast telephone dialling, simultaneous publication of national news media, and jet transport. The result is that Americans share in common many daily experiences as a national community, with the same retail chains, the same network news programmes, the same televised sports events, the same type of large employers, either business or government. For those many Americans who have become rootless through frequent job transfers, the experiences of national community may be more frequent and real than experiences of local community. This coalescence into a national society has profound political implications. It has led to efforts towards national rather than regional and local solutions to social problems and, by definition, the expansion of central government into the field of social policy. This we will return to later when we discuss the nature and quality of this public intervention. Increasing population mobility within a nationwide framework also has its social consequences, the repetition of smaller-scale communities offering coherent life styles in each of the nation's urban regions, and these too will be discussed later.

At the same time that a national society has emerged, there has been a distinct structural change in the American economy—the transition to a post-industrial phase. According to Daniel Bell (1968), the post-industrial economy can be outlined schematically along five dimensions : the creation of a service economy; the pre-eminence of the professional and technical class; the centrality of theoretical knowledge as the source of innovation and policy formulation in society; the possibility of self-sustaining technological growth and transformation; and the emergence of a new intellectual technology centring on information and information-processing, leading to the growth of a quaternary sector in the economy. Such ingredients of a post-industrial economy tend to be 'footloose' rather than transport-oriented either to raw materials or markets, and they use high-grade highly skilled high-priced labour. Amenities for this labour—the preferred residential settings that support the desired life style—loom ever larger in their locational decisions. The employees form part of a national rather than any local labour market. And the nature of the talent used is such that it is the source of the new ideas that breed further growth.

As growth has taken place, links between social and spatial mobility have been reinforced by a peculiarly American social dynamic. David McClelland (1962) has pointed out that the drive for achievement is a variable of key importance within the 'mainstream' American culture—a culture in which status and self-respect come from what a person *does*, in the material world, rather than from his ancestry or his holiness. Social and spatial mobility are built into and interrelated within individuals' nervous systems as a result of the attitudes and pressures of the culture. There is a continual need to compete with an internalised standard of excellence. Children must 'get ahead' and 'improve themselves' through education. Workers must ascend the job hierarchy. Earnings must be spent on the best possible homes and material possessions in the best possible neighbourhoods. Any increase in job or financial status must be matched by a move to a better neighbourhood in which the new and higher-status life style may be pursued. 'Downgrading' of the neighbourhood through entry of those perceived to be of lower status must be fought, and if the perceived external threat cannot be contained one must flee to avoid the inevitable resulting loss of status. To do otherwise would be to abandon the aggressive pursuit and the outward display of 'success'; one must always 'fight' to 'win'.

When a family seeks a home they look for other things too, of course. The prime decision relates to the home—its price and type,

determined by achieved status and by the family's needs at the
stage in its life cycle that the choice is made. Since a large number
of homes qualify within these first bounds for all but the poor,
neighbourhood considerations then come into play. The scale of
urban regions has brought complexity and the rapidity of urban
change produces uncertainty and insecurity. The whole is too large
for the individual to comprehend. In the search for self-identity
in a mass society, he seeks to minimise disorder by living in a
neighbourhood in which life is comprehensible and social relations predictable. Indeed, he moves out of 'his' neighbourhood
when he can no longer predict the consequences of a particular
pattern of behaviour. He seeks an enclave of relative homogeneity : a predictable life style; a territory free from status competition because his neighbours are 'just like him'; a turf
compatible in outlook because his neighbours are at similar stages
in the life cycle; a safe area, free from status-challenging ethnic
or racial minorities; a haven from complexity, to be protected
and safeguarded by whatever means—legal, institutional, and
frequently illegal violence, each a symptom of defensive terri-
toriality protecting that which has been achieved.

The resulting homogeneous niches are exquisitely reticulated
in geographic space. High-status neighbourhoods seek out zones
of superior residential amenity near water, trees, and higher
ground, free from the risk of floods and away from smoke and
factories, and increasingly in the furthest accessible peripheries.
Middle-status neighbourhoods press as close to the high-status as
feasible. To the low-status resident, least able to afford costs of
commuting, are relinquished the least desirable areas adjacent to
industrial zones radiating from the centre of the city along rail-
roads and rivers, the zones of highest pollution and the oldest,
most deteriorated homes. From these areas the poor, too, aspire to
depart, and are now doing so in increasing numbers, leaving behind widening zones of housing abandonment in the hearts of
the central cities.

These dynamics are fed by an extremely efficient suburban
housing industry. The 1970 census showed there to be 69 million
housing units in the United States, whereas there had been 46
million in 1950. Of the 69 million, 30.5 million were constructed
in the period 1950–70, during which time the net addition of
households was only 20.4 million. The aggregate number of sub-

standard units fell in the same period by 70 per cent, from 17 to 5 million. Space standards per person reached new highs while crowding reached new lows. The number of units that lack complete private plumbing facilities decreased to only 8 per cent in 1970—mostly in rural areas. The number of overcrowded units— as indicated by the number of units averaging more than one person per room—decreased from 16 per cent in 1950 to 12 per cent in 1960 to 8 per cent in 1970. The median size of household decreased from 3·1 in 1950 to 3·0 in 1960 to 2·7 in 1970. Almost two-thirds of American families are home-owners and single-family homes still account for over two-thirds of the housing inventory. More housing was produced in 1971 than ever in the nation's history.

Obviously, the outmigration of middle and higher income families has been made possible by the availability of better housing in a better living environment in developing suburban areas. High housing production rates are, therefore, a factor in the outmigration of families from older, declining, poor living environment neighbourhoods of the cities. The development of new suburban housing provides the living alternative many city residents seek. In turn, new construction at rates exceeding the rate of growth of demand also produces 'filtering', exerting downward pressures on rents and prices of existing housing and permitting lower income families to obtain better housing. The filtering extends downwards in complex chains of successive moves, with the vacancies that develop at each step filled by lower income families moving from the poorer and more adequate neighbourhoods in the city. At the end of the chain, the working poor find they can move on to other housing, leaving behind concentrations of the very poorest families, many of whom have serious problems, and who, supported by welfare, have little hope of upward mobility. The poorest areas of the cities with the heaviest concentrations of the 'pathological' poor become abandoned by all others. There are no longer any takers for the old, decayed units that are left. In New York, where the process has moved furthest, 105,000 housing units were abandoned in 1971.

Racial discrimination adds another dimension to the filtering process in U.S. cities—a push rather than a pull. Black families, Chicano (Spanish American) families, minorities moving into vacancies in a white area, accelerate the outmigration of whites.

migration flow fed by threat to security.

The first minority families moving into such neighbourhoods pay for quality in housing. But fear of racial change and eventual racial concentration makes mobile whites move out faster, and continued racial separation of neighbourhoods is the result. To illustrate, if we plot in a graph, for each of the central cities of U.S. metropolitan areas, the rate of population change on one axis, and the number of percentage points by which the black population increased in the same period on the other axis, a clear inverse relationship appears (Fig. 9). The greater the increase in size and concentration of the ghetto, the more rapid the decrease of the central city's total population, the decrease running at about twice the rate of the black increase! These polarisation patterns, formerly varying substantially from one region of the country to another, are now nationwide in their appearance, another indication of the emergence of the national society.

here — the turf.

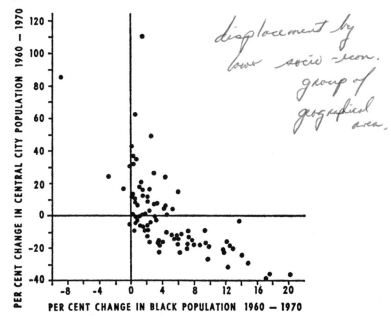

displacement by lower socio-econ. group of geographical area.

FIG. 9 The relationship between population change in U.S. central cities and growth of their black populations, 1960–70

The result is the picture of the American urban future painted by President Johnson's *Commission on Crimes of Violence*:

Contrary to Wirth + the 'Melting Pot' thesis.

We can expect further social fragmentation of the urban environment, formation of excessively parochial communities, greater segregation of different racial groups and economic classes . . . and polarisation of attitudes on a variety of issues. It is logical to expect the establishment of the 'defensive city' consisting of an economically declining central business district in the inner city protected by people shopping or working in buildings during daylight hours and 'sealed off' by police during nighttime hours. Highrise apartment buildings and residential 'compounds' will be fortified 'cells' for upper-, middle-, and high-income populations living at prime locations in the inner city. Suburban neighbourhoods, geographically removed from the central city, will be 'safe areas', protected mainly by racial and economic homogeneity . . .

Again, the idea of social isolation within metropolitan regions, suggested by Handlin, is raised, alongside the emergence of the national society, and it is the links between the two that must be forged into the new social theory that is needed to comprehend new ways of life in new urban systems.

Cause of density

The concentrated industrial metropolis only developed because proximity meant lower transportation and communication costs for those interdependent specialists who had to interact with each other frequently or intensively. One of the most important forces contributing to the new urbanisation is the erosion of centrality by time–space convergence. Virtually all the technological developments of industrial times have had the effect of reducing the constraints of geographic space. Developments in transportation and communications have made it possible for each generation to live farther from activity centres and for information users to rely upon information sources that are spatially distant.

reverse trend

Contemporary developments in communications are supplying better channels for transmitting information and improving the capacities of partners in social intercourse to transact their business at great distances. It was the demand for ease of communication that first brought men into cities. The time-eliminating properties of long-distance communication and the space-spanning capacities of the new communications technologies are combining to concoct a solvent that has dissolved the core-oriented city in both time and space, creating what some refer to as 'an urban civilisation without cities' (Kristol, 1972).

What is being focused on is what J.-J. Servan-Schreiber (1967) has called the essence of 'The American Challenge', the compression of time and space and the acceleration of change, with intensification of human experience alongside lessening demands for face-to-face contact because of the centralised information sources and instantaneous communication which are producing a quality of presence in the transactions of distant partners in a variety of space-eroding ways. The revolutionary aspect of the new electronic technologies is that they not only reduce the frictions in moving goods and people; they can move the experience instead to the human nervous system. Traditionally, we have moved the body to the experience; increasingly we will have the option to move the experience to the body. The body can, therefore, be located where it finds the non-electronic experiences most satisfying, and thus the second part of the change—increasing localism.

Already population is trending accordingly. Settlement patterns are spreading broadly over the continental surface, localised at those places where the climate and landscape are most pleasant. Densities are settling down at the scale of the exurban fringes of the Eastern metropolitan areas. The edges of many of the nation's daily urban systems have now pushed one hundred miles and more from the traditional city centres. More important, the core-orientation implied in use of the terms 'central city' is fast on the wane. Today's daily urban systems appear to be multi-nodal multi-connected social systems in action. The essence of any such system is its linkages and interactions, as changed by changing modes of communication. Both place of residence and place of work are seen to be responding to social dynamics. At the same time, new communications media, notably television, have contributed to the universal perception in the United States of decaying central cities, the new home of the former residents of the now-emptied periphery; the immediate on-the-spot experience of their riots; the careful documentation of their frustrations; and acute awareness of emerging separatist feelings. It is no accident that the suburbanisation of white city-dwellers has increased, supported by rising real incomes and increased leisure time, as persons of greater wealth and leisure seek homes and work among the more remote environments of hills, water and forest, while most aspire to such an ideal. It is the spontaneous creation of new communities, the flows that respond to new transportation arteries, the waves emanating from growth centres, the mutually repulsive interactions of antagonistic social groups, the reverse commuting resulting from increasing segregation along city boundary lines as employment decentralises, and many other facets of social dynamics that have combined to create America's new urban systems. The situation is very different from the period at the end of the nineteenth century from which was derived the traditional concept of urbanisation.

TOWARDS A NEW SOCIAL THEORY

As yet no new social theory has been developed to account for the dynamics of this new urbanisation in America and to explain its human consequences. At its minimum, such a theory must comprehend the tension between increasing scale and mobility in a truly national society on the one hand and increasing insistence upon a mosaic of small and coherent communities with predictable life styles within a context of intensifying cultural pluralism on the other.

Janet Abu-Lughod (1968) points out that despite the fact that earlier terminologies are proving inadequate, it might be possible to develop the needed theory by substituting scale, interactional density and internal differentiation for Wirth's causal trilogy of size, density and heterogeneity. Let us look at these alternative variables.

Scale and Mobility

Scale differs from size, according to Abu-Lughod, in that it measures the extent of a given network of relationships, not the number of its participants, although as extent widens the number of persons directly or indirectly affected by system decisions naturally increases. What is missing from the concept of scale is a clear geographic referent. Whereas in the urbanism described by Wirth scale was geographically coterminous with size, in the new urbanism it is not, because what is involved in an increase in nationwide mobility.

Another American sociologist, Scott Greer (1962), has identified three aspects of increasing societal scale that are of major importance. The widening of the radii of interdependence means that, whether men know it or not, they become mutual means to individual ends; the intensity of interdependence increases. As a concomitant, increasing scale produces an increasing range and content of the communications flow. This results in a widening span of compliance and control within given social organisations, the salience of large-scale organisations, their nationwide span of control, and the similarity of their division of labour and rewards, tending to develop a stratification system cutting across widely varying geographical and cultural sub-regions of the country, creating *national citizens*.

This nationwide quality, together with its accompaniment, increasing mobility, has been highlighted by Vance Packard (1972). Packard finds that the average American moves 14 times in his lifetime, compared to 8 for a Briton, 6 for a Frenchman, 5 for the Japanese. However, the rates are quite different for different social groups. The high mobiles are those with some college education, higher incomes, working for large corporate or governmental organisations, in the mid-twenty to mid-forty age span. The low mobiles are the blue collar employees and other working-class people, whose lives are built around kinship and ethnic ties within local neighbourhoods. When the high mobiles move, it involves a shift from one urban region to another, but in moving they scarcely change their life style; there is a tendency to move between near-identical social environments, and indeed, their assessment of the quality of life in a community centres on the characteristics of its social environment. Professional real estate consultants aid them in their search for communities that offer the same environment in terms of schools and neighbours, income levels, education, family background and clubs. Packard notes: 'They will not be changing their environment, they will just be changing their address.' The attachment to a type of environment that sustains a particular life style is the key to the way in which contemporary Americans have adjusted the need to retain a locally based sense of security and stability to the emergence of nationwide high-mobile society.

Packard equates mobility with rootlessness and rootlessness with a proneness to malaise. Among the things he associates with the new migratory life style are low degrees of community involvement, small numbers of close friends, high rates of alcoholism and infidelity. He also suggests a much greater tendency to flee the unpleasant, and consequently, low tolerance for frustration, marked impulsiveness, and a growing tendency for misrepresentation. Like the Progressives, Packard says there is a need to recover a sense of community in America. Such perceptions are

solution to mobility & rootlessness

disputed by psychiatrists, however—for example Leo Srole (1972). Srole shows that even if in the past mental disorder frequencies were higher in cities, new evidence shows that this no longer obtains. No longer, he argues, should such place-bound variables as size or density be used to compare mental disorder rates, because mobility implies for many higher mobiles at least four successive life-styles in significantly different physical settings : growing up in a smaller community; career building in the apartment neighbourhoods of a city; child-raising in a suburb; and retirement by 'empty nest' couples to better climates, to exurb country places, or to exclusive big-city apartment complexes. In this sense, then, the type of community occupied is not an antecedent causal variable, but a self-selected and interactive or circular variable related to life-style preferences. Further, during the rhythms of daily activity, the adult experiences many types of communities. The basic question from the viewpoint of mental health thus becomes : What kinds of people differentially stay in or are drawn to various kinds of milieus? And Srole concludes from his Midtown Manhattan Study (1962) that for *children* under special conditions of parental psychopathology, economic poverty and family disorganisation, both metropolitan and rural slums are more psychopathogenic than adjoining non-slum neighbourhoods; and for *adults* seeking a change in environment, the metropolis under most conditions is a more therapeutic milieu than the smaller community, especially for nonconformists and escapee-deviants.

Interactional Density

Abu-Lughod argued that density also requires a redefinition to make it applicable to twentieth-century urbanism. She noted that Durkheim, while making a conceptual distinction between material density (population concentration) and dynamic density (rate of interaction), could still conclude that if the technology for increasing social contacts were taken into consideration, material density could be used as an index to dynamic density. This congruence, which Wirth's investigation of urbanism assumed, has been breaking apart. Interactional density facilitated by communication is far greater than physical density permits or requires, as Richard Meier reveals clearly enough (1962).

Yet Abu-Lughod goes further, and it will be useful to repeat her argument. This new density, she says, is different in *kind* than the interactions that were measured indirectly through concentration. Increasingly, interaction on primary and secondary levels of involvement is being supplemented by a form of interaction even more abstracted from the deeper layers of personality : *tertiary interactions* leading to tertiary relationships. If a primary relationship is one in which the individuals are known to each other in many role facets whereas a secondary relationship implies a knowledge of the other individual only in a single role facet, then a tertiary relationship is one in which only the *roles* interact. The individuals playing the roles are interchangeable and, in fact, with the computerisation of many interactions, are even dispensable, at least at the point of immediate contact. What are interacting are not *individuals* in one role capacity or another but the functional roles themselves. Such tertiary relationships can *only* be maintained under conditions of *physical* isolation; once supplemented by physical contact, they tend to revert to the secondary. Thus, the isolation of different communities within urban regions promotes role and life-style stereotyping via perceptions created by mass media imagery, particularly television, and many people behave to others as if these perceptions are correct.

Internal Differentiation
In Wirth's view, heterogeneity arose primarily from external sources, and was continually reinforced and sustained by migration. The city, which brought into contact persons of diverse backgrounds, was conceived of as a fertile soil for cross-pollination; physical mobility was presumed to lead to mental mobility, i.e., cosmopolitanism and a questioning of inherited beliefs. The local community was conceived as being bound together primarily by bonds of sentiment rather than the instrumental usefulness of residents to one another, and these bonds were felt to be weaker in the city than in small towns. Within cities, Robert Park's image of a 'sorting-out process', into 'little worlds that touch but do not interpenetrate', prevailed. The city was thought of as a mosaic of village-like units which stayed to themselves and closely controlled their members. Park, like other Progressive thinkers, looked back to the days of the family, the tribe and the clan with some sense of nostalgia, and he looked to communications, education and new forms of politics to reconstitute communities of sentiment and

create a social order equivalent to that which grew up naturally in the simpler types of society, a positive outcome of heterogeneity and the melting-pot. But Wirth and his contemporaries felt that the growth of large-scale organisations, centralisation of organisational control, increasing functional division of labour and widespread use of the automobile were all reducing the significance of the local community. Neither the predicted decline in heterogeneity nor increasing homegeneity through blending in the 'melting pot' have occurred, however; rather, the coalescence of society has facilitated an elaborate internal subdivision.

First, the extent to which many of the immigrant groups have been assimilated into the larger society now appears to be quite limited. Milton M. Gordon (1964) sees the process of assimilation as involving several steps or sub-processes. Each step represents a 'type' or 'stage' in the assimilation process. He identifies seven variables by which one may gauge the degree to which members of a particular group are assimilated into the host society which surrounds them. The stages and sub-processes are:

Type or Stage of Assimilation	*Sub-process or Condition*
1. Cultural or behavioural assimilation	Change in cultural patterns to those of host society
2. Structural assimilation	Large-scale entrance into cliques, clubs, and institutions of host society on primary-group level
3. Marital assimilation	Large-scale intermarriage
4. Identificational assimilation	Development of a sense of peoplehood based exclusively on host society
5. Attitude receptional assimilation	Absence of prejudice
6. Behavioural receptional assimilation	Absence of discrimination
7. Civic assimilation	Absence of value or power conflict

Using this sequence, White Protestant Americans are the most assimilated; indeed, it is they who most frequently constitute the mainstream or host society (Anderson, 1970). Yet in primary group life, even they tend to clique. Much of the New England upper class has consisted, for example, of a group of self-conscious Yankee families clustered in their own exclusive social institutions.

At the other extreme, Black Americans display mimimal assimilation (Pinkney, 1969). They are by and large acculturated, but
there is minimal structural, marital and identificational assimilation. They continue to experience widespread prejudice and discrimination, and conflicts are increasing rather than decreasing
as Black Power advocates achieve a broader constituency. Where
there have been deliberate attempts to integrate, as with busing
school children, racial frictions have escalated and the result has
been greater polarisation rather than increased tolerance (Armor,
1972).

Jewish Americans have become a thoroughly Americanised
group, acculturated to the American middle-class way of life
(Goldstein, 1968). Yet, at the same time, there is an increasing
emphasis on 'being Jewish', including association with Jewish
culture, religion and organisational life. Third and later generation Jews, in particular, are seeking to temper assimilation with
separate group identity.

As for other groups, Japanese Americans have experienced the
pluralistic development of a congruent Japanese culture within the
larger American society (Kitano, 1969), while for both Indian and
Mexican Americans there remains a bifurcation of subculture
and White (Wax, 1971; Moore, 1970), increasing because of the
militancy of the 'Red Power' and Chicano movements.

In the case of other ethnic groups, especially the blue-collar
eastern and southern European Catholics, expressions of cultural
pluralism are increasing, too. Let us focus on Chicago as an example. Race and ethnicity now dominate the public life of Chicago. Chicago's residential patterns, neighbourhood schools, shops,
community newspapers, hospitals, old-age homes, cemeteries, saving and loan associations, charitable, fraternal and cultural
organisations attest to the role of ethnicity in Chicago's culture
and politics. Public decisions affecting home ownership, schools,
public housing, police, shopkeepers, allocation of state and
federal funds and welfare are increasingly perceived in terms of
nationality-group or racial-group attachments. Ethnicity defines
interest groups in the city, is recognised in the public decision-making of the city, and is rewarded and encouraged by the politicians
and established institutions. Ethnic and racial quotas have been
informally adopted by public officials on a large scale. The formation in Chicago of associations of policemen and public school-

teachers along ethnic and racial lines, and the revitalisation of ethnic and racial vocational and professional associations, confirm the trend to define interests in these terms.

When the heterogeneity of American cities was caused primarily by the influx of successive immigrant waves, the policy of encouraging assimilation was taken for granted ideologically. Consumers might demonstrate a wide range of behaviours and preferences, but this variety was viewed as being both temporary and expendable. A white, middle-class 'Americanised' standard could be imposed from the outside and justified in terms of the shared higher goal of assimilation. People behaved the way they did only because they had not yet *learned* the better way. The segregated local residential community was regarded as a passing entity which might be maintained only so long as temporary patterns of racial and socio-economic segregation persisted, but ultimately the local community would decline as people found other, preferable, non-territorial bases for association. Territorial groups were, it was felt, coercive in character and far less attractive than voluntary forms of association. The latter would shortly replace local community ties and these 'interest communities' would result in a more faithful response from government and big business. The local community would decline then as racial and socio-economic segregation declined and interest communities replaced residential communities.

What is indicated in American urban regions today is, however, that a new type of heterogeneity exists and is intensifying. This hetereogeneity results from internal differentiation and may be understood from the different ideological position of cultural pluralism. In such a framework, the forms of community that emerge are in no way vestigial remnants of a more fragmented localised society.

A major advance in understanding these new forms of community has been made by Gerald Suttles (1972). Suttles argues that a useful point at which to begin is by retrieving the cognitive maps of childhood. For the child, awareness of the city radiates outward, with the density of information diminishing rapidly with the distance from home. The area of comfortable familiarity constitutes the experience of neighbourhood.

Yet cities do not consist of an infinitely large number of neighbourhoods each centring on one of millions of inhabitants only a slight spatial remove from his fellows. Rather there is a small number of social labels applied to definable geographic areas. Because population characteristics of a city are continuously variable, with no clear demarcation between one side of the street and the other, society imposes categorical labels on specific geographic realms. Neighbourhood categories are not simply found in nature, but are consensually imposed definitions.

A neighbourhood label, once affixed, has real consequences, Suttles points out. For outsiders it reduces decision-making to more manageable terms. Instead of dealing with the variegated reality of numerous city streets, the resident can form a set of attitudes about a limited number of social categories and act accordingly. For those who live within it, the neighbourhood defines areas relatively free of intruders, identifies where potential friends are to be found or where they are to be cultivated, minimises the prospects of status insult, and simplifies innumerable daily decisions dealing with spatial activities. Thus the mental map of neighbourhoods is not superfluous cognitive baggage, but performs important psychological and social functions.

In Suttles' scheme, the boundaries of neighbourhoods are set by physical barriers, ethnic homogeneity, social class and other factors that together contribute to the definition of homogeneous areas that are supportive of particular life styles. But if a neighbourhood exists first as a creative social construction, it nonetheless possesses a number of important properties. First, it becomes a component of an individual's identity, a stable judgmental reference against which people are assessed. A neighbourhood may derive its reputation from several sources: first, from the master identity of the area of which it is a part; second, through comparison and contrast with adjacent communities; and third, from historic claims. In this framework, the idea of a community as first and foremost a group of people bound together by common sentiments, a primordial solidarity, represents an over-romanticised view of social life. Communities do lead to social control, they do segregate people to avoid danger, insult, and status claims; but whatever sentiments are engendered by neighbourhoods are strictly tied to functional realities.

There are multiple levels of community organisation in which the resident participates. The smallest of these units is the *face block*. For children it is the prescribed social world carved out by parents. It is here that face-to-face relations are most likely, and the resulting institutional form is the block association. Next, in Suttles' typology, is the *defended neighbourhood* or *minimal named community*, which is the smallest segment of the city recognised by both residents and outsiders as possessing a particular character, and which possesses many of the facilities needed to carry out the daily routine of life. Third, the urban resident also participates in the *community of limited liability*, a larger realm possessing an institutionally secure name and boundaries. The concept, originally developed by Morris Janowitz (1952), emphasises the intentional, voluntary, and especially the differential involvement of residents in their local communities. Frequently an external agent, such as a community newspaper, is the most important guardian of such a community's sense of boundaries, purpose, and integrity. Finally, even larger segments of the city may also take shape in response to environmental pressures, creating an *expanded community of limited liability*. Thus an individual may find himself picketing to keep a highway not just out of his neighbourhood, but out of the entire South Side. In this way, varied levels of community organisation are created as responses to the larger social environment. The urban community mirrors the social differentiation of the total society.

Life Styles in the Mosaic Culture

The communities in which Americans thus live vary in their racial, ethnic, and socio-economic composition and thus in their available life styles; in their physical features, which can be used to create images and boundaries; and in their historic claims to a distinct reputation or identity. Members of a mobile society select among communities in terms of the life style they are perceived to offer. What, then, are some of the principal life-style differences that are to be found within American society today, setting aside the differentiation associated with cultural intensification based on race and ethnicity?

They appear to arise from the experience by all Americans of two common developmental processes : (1) passage through stages of the life cycle, with especially sharp breaks associated with the transition from one state to another, as in marriage, family expansion, entry into the labour force, retirement, etc.; and (2) occupational career trajectories that may necessitate, preclude, or otherwise pattern geographic mobility alongside social mobility. These developmental processes are cross-cut by several different value systems : *familism*, in which a high value is placed upon family living and a corresponding devotion of time and resources to family life; *careerism*, in which there is an orientation toward upward social mobility and a corresponding disposition to engage in career-related activities, at least to a partial neglect of family ties; *localism*, a parochial orientation implying interests confined to a neighbourhood and reference to groups whose scope is local; and *cosmopolitanism*, an ecumenical orientation implying freedom from the binding ties to a locality and reference to groups whose scope is national rather than local, so that the cosmopolitan resides in a place but inhabits the nation.

From these bases, one can distinguish between *working-class communities*, *ghettos* and *ethnic centres* where the broad pattern of interaction is one where informal meeting places, street corner gangs, church groups and precinct politics tend to dominate the collective forms of communal life; *middle income, familistic areas*, in which informal relations seem to be heavily shaped by the management of children, and formal organisations are much more extensively developed than in lower income areas; the *affluent apartment complex* and the *exclusive suburb*, which generally have a privatised mode of interaction and organisation : social clubs, private schools, country clubs and businessmen's associations; and *cosmopolitan centres*, which have long existed in some cities and which seem to be sprouting up in other cities as they grow and are able to provide a critical mass of local grown talent and misfits, to create their own symbiotic milieus of tolerance (Suttles, 1972).

Quoting Fischer (1972), in the latter cases emerge the most extreme forms of *subcultural intensification*—the strengthening of the beliefs, values and cohesion both of groups that previously existed as social entities outside the city, and of new groups emerging within expanding urban systems as new cultural values and norms are established. Two ingredients are involved: growth of " 'critical masses' such that subcultural institutions can develop (e.g. political power and national churches for ethnic groups; hangouts for 'bohemians'; bookstores for intellectuals; museums for artists; new communities for the elderly; and 'turfs' for each group) which strengthen the subculture and attract more of its members to the city"; and "contrasts with other subcultures that intensify people's identification with and adherence to their own. Whereas Wirth thought that the clash of different values in the city might negate all values, it appears that internal cohesion is strengthened by the conflict that arises on contact." Such, for example, is David Armor's conclusion in 'The Evidence on Busing' (1972).

One important form of intensification is that appearing in criminal subcultures. Whereas the Wirthian model explains deviance by the breakdown of norms, the alternative is to see deviance as constituting *subcultural* deviance from centre-society values. The group nature of much crime, especially urban crime, seems clear. The State of Illinois classifies its prison population into four subgroups, for example : the socio-pathetic, the immature, the neurotic and the gang-related, with the latter the largest group. Greater criminality in cities might, therefore, be explained by an intensification process for criminals (e.g. growth of an underground), as well as an intensification process for criminals' targets (i.e. the concentration of wealth and the wealthy). The same intensification process would operate in regard to other deviant subcultures : homosexuals, prostitutes, 'hippies', political dissidents, etc.

What appears to have emerged and to be emerging in America as a result of these changes is a *mosaic culture*—a society with a number of parallel and distinctively different life styles. While one result is divisive tendencies for the society as a whole, at another level, mutual harmony is produced by mutual withdrawal into homogeneous communities, exclusion and isolation from groups with different life styles and values. A mosaic of homogeneous communities maintains different life styles that are internally cohesive and exclusive, but externally non-aggressive unless threatened. Mobility within the mosaic leads to a high degree of expressed satisfaction by residents with their communities, and the option for those who are dissatisfied to move to an alternative that is more in keeping with their life-style requirements (Gans, 1968).

THE AMERICAN PLANNING STYLE

As this twentieth-century transformation of urbanisation has been unfolding, the American planning style has tended to be supportive of privatism and the mosaic culture rather than productive of alternative urban futures.

New Towns in the United States

Consider the U.S. experience with the construction of new towns. The first of these, dating from before the twentieth century, were company towns to serve industrial enterprises. Later came planned suburban developments established to capture the residential spin-off from large cities. Around the First World War the Federal Government established a number of emergency housing communities in industrial areas. During the 1920s some efforts were made to create American garden cities patterned after Letchworth in England. The most notable examples are a series of communities designed by Clarence Stein, although most of these were only planned areas within a larger city, as in the case of Sunnyside Gardens in New York City (1924-8) and Chatham Village in Pittsburgh (1932) The first community actually started as an independent garden city was Radburn, New Jersey (some 16 miles from New York City), which was begun in 1928.

During the New Deal in the 1930s serious attention was given to creating a number of new towns, the Greenbelt Towns, under Federal Government auspices. Rexford G. Tugwell, the programme administrator, wanted to build 3000. Twenty-five were selected by the Resettlement Administration. President Roosevelt approved 8 of these, and Congress reduced the number to 5. Finally, only 3—Greenbelt, Maryland; Greenhills, Ohio; and Greendale, Wisconsin—were ever built (Conkin, 1959; Arnold, 1971). In addition, the Federal Government became involved in new town development in the 1930s in connection with a number of large-scale power and reclamation projects and in the 1940s through its atomic energy programme.

One recent study has found that a total of 376 urban developments of 950 acres or more, using nearly 1.5 million acres of land, were started in the United States between 1960 and 1967. Of these, 43 could be classified by the survey as new towns, mainly located in areas of rapid growth and warm weather. The builders of all these new town projects have been called 'the new entrepreneurs'. They include (1) *builder-developers* with a real estate and home-building background; (2) *large national corporations* interested in product promotion and financial diversification; (3) *large landowners* looking for a way to increase the value of property originally acquired for other purposes, such as for farming or mining; and (4) the big *mortgage lenders*, such as banks, insurance companies, and savings and loan associations, as well as a rare independent developer, who enters the field more or less by accident. The important thing to note about all of these groups is that they are *private*. American new town development is explicitly entrepreneurial, exploiting the profit-making potentialities latent in urban growth and change. To the extent that there is public involvement, it involves reducing the risk to the entrepreneur in exchange for some mild regulation of the development style.

On occasions, the result is of high quality. Reston, Virginia, and Columbia, Maryland, are certainly the two most highly publicised examples of privately built new towns in the United States. Reston has attracted a good deal of attention for its efforts at preserving the great natural beauty of its site and for its high quality in architectural design. Columbia has made a definite effort to attrack black residents, has explored federal programmes for providing low-cost housing for the poor, has shown considerable interest in the sociology of urban development, yet has also been challenged by local resident interest groups as it has grown, on issues of corporate paternalism. Nonetheless, recent research indicates that residents of Reston and Columbia rate both their communities and their micro-neighbourhoods more highly than residents of less-planned suburbs rate theirs (a finding that has been repeated elsewhere, for example in Britain's New Towns), and indeed, in many cases the concept and planning were the attractions leading to the initial move in. Among the important features appear to be the adequacy and location of open spaces for family activities that wind as sinews through the residential areas of both towns, the lower noise levels, and the superior maintenance levels. Along with quality of the schools, the greatest sources of satisfaction with planned communities relate to the environment (Zehner, 1972).

Housing Policy

Much the same story can be told about U.S. housing policy. Recall that the Federal Housing Administration (FHA) has been created as part of the New Deal's efforts to insure mortgages under certain circumstances, to eliminate the worst housing, to provide public housing for the poor, and above all, to help in priming the pump of the economy. By 1950 170,000 dwellings had been provided for low-income families.

Programme development following the Second World War was additive. To the FHA were added the mortgage assistance programmes of the Veterans Administration that ultimately were taken advantage of by more than 6.8 million returning veterans seeking new homes. The Housing Act of 1949 strengthened and extended the slum clearance and public housing programmes, to be followed by later acts that created the workable programme for community improvement as the prerequisite to housing assistance and urban renewal (1954), the community renewal (1959) and model cities programmes, progressively moving towards comprehensive socio-economic as well as physical goals for the cities. Even more comprehensive enactments came in 1968 and 1970, leaving the United States not simply with a Department of Housing and Urban Development, but with a 'New Communities' programme, too. And many other public investment programmes have materially affected the urban scene, most notably the massive Interstate Highway Programme, but including a host of others, including airports, sewage systems, recreation and open space facilities, and hospitals.

Federal housing programmes contributed to the suburbanisation of America in important ways, creating hundreds of standardised 'Levittowns'. In these developments, federal policy combined with local planning to maintain and support neighbourhood homogeneity, and specifically to exclude the Black and the poor. We referred in Chapter 1 to the conservatism of American zoning. In city planning practice in the inter- and immediate post-war periods one of the most influential ideas was Clarence Perry's 'Neighbourhood Unit' concept. Perry felt it important that cities be built up of sharply bounded neighbourhood units, physically distinctive, and possessing local unity by virtue of organisation around a shared focus of community activity. Perry's model had a profound influence on local planning commissions and zoning boards. The idea that well-designed neighbourhoods would bring about social cohesiveness, neighbourliness, and the virtues of the small community within the large city was consistent with the dominant social philosophy; associated was the belief in the necessity of maintaining neighbourhood homogeneity : an 'incompatible mix' referred to different racial, ethnic groups as much as to industrial activity in residential areas. Mixture of racial and cultural groups, in particular, was considered detrimental to the neighbourhood. Restrictive covenants explicitly excluded members of minority groups. The National Association of Real Estate Board's 'code of ethics' made it unethical for a realtor to introduce 'incompatible' groups to a neighbourhood. Early editions of the FHA Appraisers' Handbook forbade social integration, and demanded that mortgage institutions follow suit. The suburbanisation of the white middle class and the ghettoisation of the poor and minorities in the central city implied thereby were not creations of federal policy—residential segregation and sub-community formation date at least to the early nineteenth century—but they certainly were promoted by federal activity in the post-war years.

Emergence of Broader Concepts of Urban Development

With the 1960s came a search for a new comprehensiveness in the federal approach to urban problems (Scott, 1969). Part of the switch was one of emphasis, from plan-making to planning as a process; part involved recognition of the need to orchestrate physical and social programmes in the central cities if a significant impact was to be made on the pockets of poverty in the ghettos. Such efforts as the Community Renewal Programme and the Model Cities Programme were launched. The most significant development came in the Housing Act of 1968. This act confirmed growing disaffection with the pace of housing starts for the poor, and provided new programmes that produced 300,000 new low-income housing units in the years 1968–70, raising the low-income proportion of total housing starts from 3 per cent in 1961 to 16 per cent in 1971 (Kristof, 1972). A parallel debate on national growth policy culminated in 1970 with the passage of title VII of the Housing and Urban Development Act, requiring the President

in order to assist in the development of a national urban policy . . . to transmit to the Congress during the month of February in every even-numbered year beginning with 1972, a Report on Urban Growth.

The first such report was President Nixon's Domestic Council *Report on National Growth 1972*, which concluded that, in the United States, privatism should prevail :

Patterns of growth are influenced by countless decisions made by individuals, families and businesses ... aimed at achieving the personal goals of those who make them ... [Such] decisions cannot be dictated. ... In many nations, the central government has undertaken forceful, comprehensive policies to control the process of growth. Similar policies have not been adopted in the United States for several reasons. Among the most important is the distinctive form of government which we value so highly ... it is not feasible for the highest level of government to design policies for development that can operate successfully in all parts of the nation.

Earlier, in 1968 President Nixon had created a National Goals Research Staff, and assigned three functions to it: forecasting future developments, and assessing longer-range consequences of present social trends; measuring the probable future impact of alternative courses of action; and estimating the actual range of social choice, indicating what alternative sets of goals might be attainable in terms of available resources and possible rates of progress. He was also interested in having it develop devices 'that enable us to assess where we stand and are going with respect to our values and goals, and to evaluate specific programmes and determine their impact'. Surely, it was thought, better statistics of direct normative interest would help us make balanced, comprehensive and concise judgments about the conditions of society. Surely we would benefit if, as many have said, we 'apply real science to social affairs', thus eliminating the corruptions of the principle of rationality that arise when decisions about social affairs are made on the basis of beliefs about facts, rather than 'true knowledge'. Yet the Staff's report on *National Growth: Quantity with Quality* has been widely acknowledged to be a dismal failure.

The Problem of Pluralism
What had been ignored by the Staff were the multiple and competing interest groups in American society. American society, like any other democratic pluralistic society (for America we could substitute Australia or Canada without loss of generality), is inherently incapable of being goal-oriented for deep-seated reasons; the future, instead, is likely to be an outgrowth of present processes, as regulated by legal devices to preserve 'mainstream' values, while subject to the possibility of major transformations produced not by design, but by major entrepreneurial decisions made in the private

sector or carried out by the govenment at the behest of powerful private lobbying interests.

One consequence is to be seen in American political science, in which there has developed an explicit belief system concerning the process by which policies change, which in turn influences the way in which a problem is perceived. The dominant mode of thought on this subject in American political science is that of *incrementalism*. As Charles E. Lindbloom says (1963) : 'Democracies change their policies almost entirely through incremental adjustments. Policy does not move in leaps and bounds.' The political processes of bargaining, log-rolling, and coalition-building are, of course, the major factors producing a situation in which past decisions are the best predictors of future ones.

Under such pressures, the applied rationality of goal-oriented national planning presents fundamental challenges to the traditional decision-making style. To cite one example, the politician who remains in power by manipulating interest-group politics and dispensing patronage feels severely challenged by goal-oriented activity because the very utility of future-oriented planning is to provide a basis for decision-making more rational than that of interest-group politics.

Similarly, in Canada N. H. Lithwick (1970) notes that no explicit policy guides urban growth. Impetus for urban growth derives rather from Canadians' preoccupation with economic achievement. He notes that Canada has specific economic goals such as growth, full employment, and rising levels of income which are recognised and accepted by government, labour unions, agriculture and business. Urban policy serves those economic goals, providing education, roads, utilities and supplying public housing, welfare, protective services. But this limits urban planning to an ameliorative problem-solving role, which is reinforced by an attitude that accepts the *inevitability* of a continuation of the processes inherent in the present. 'Because', Lithwick notes, 'these processes are abstract and powerful, and have served the needs of those groups who have benefited most, there is great pressure not to tamper with them.' Thus, he comes to the *'inescapable conclusion that of all [Canadian] urban problems, the one most likely to deter any major improvement is [the] urban policy problem. [The] first priority is thus not what urban policy to follow, but an agreement that any urban policy is needed'* [italics added].

No governmental bodies can be credited with the development and execution of an urban policy in Canada or the United States at the present time. What substitutes for it is a complex set of un-coordinated, often contradictory, essentially random public policies and programmes provided in the wake of strong economic forces which set the agenda for urban growth. Thus, if in the past urbanisation has been governed by any conscious public objectives at all, these have been on the one hand, to encourage growth, apparently for its own sake; and on the other, to provide public works and public welfare programmes to support piecemeal, spontaneous development impelled primarily by private initiative. In contrast, development of a national urban policy suggests a shift in the locus of initiative, imposing on public authorities an obligation to orient, rationalise, and plan the physical, economic, and textual character of urban life. Thus, through a complementary set of policies and programmes, an urban policy represents an explicit statement of the purpose of urbanisation, its pace, its character, and values that are to prevail.

Such urban policies are part of the aspirations of all Third World leaders, as we shall see in Chapter 3, but have been realised only in Europe, as we shall discover in Chapter 4.

3 Transformation During Diffusion: Third World Urbanisation

A TRANSFORMATION of the urbanisation process as profound as that in North America has been experienced in the countries of the Third World in recent decades, producing different urban forms and social consequences. Adna Weber's statistics showed urbanisation beyond Western Europe and North America to be limited in 1899 in both scale and extent to the tentacles of colonial expansion. During the twentieth century this situation has changed dramatically. As part of the quadrupling of the world's urban population during the last 50 years, the developed regions increased their urban population by a factor of 2·75 (that is, from 198 to 546 million), while the Third World countries increased their urban population by a factor of 6·75 (from 69 to 464 million). In both Latin America and Africa the urban population increased eight-fold. The big-city population of the Third World increased even faster —nine-fold—during the period 1920–60, as compared to 0·6 times for Europe and 2·4 times in other more developed regions (Table 4). Clearly it is the Third World that is experiencing the major thrust of urban growth today. With 25 per cent of the world's urban population in 1920, the Third World will encompass 51 per cent by 1980 (Davis, 1969).

THE DIFFERING CONTEXT OF URBAN GROWTH

This rapid urbanisation is taking place in the countries with the lowest levels of economic development (Fig. 10) rather than the highest, as was the case when accelerated urbanisation began in Western Europe and North America. Moreover, as Table 5 shows, it involves countries in which the people have the lowest levels of life expectancy at birth, the poorest nutritional levels, the lowest energy consumption levels and the lowest levels of education.

In the west, urbanisation involved gradual innovation and interdependent economic and social change spanning more than a century. Contemporary Third World urbanisation involves greater numbers of people than it did in the West. Migration is greater in volume, and more rapid. Industrialisation lags far behind the rate of urbanisation, so that the bulk of the migrants find at best marginal employment in the cities.

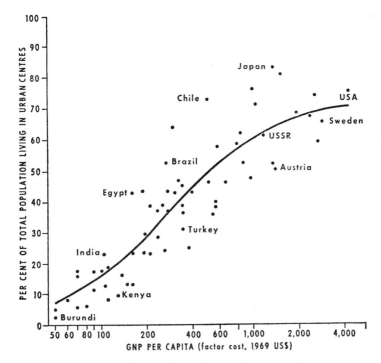

FIG. 10 Degree of urbanisation of World Bank member-countries compared with their gross national product in 1970

Graph redrawn from an original version prepared by the World Bank.

Whereas the new industrial cities in the West were death traps, the cities of the Third World are usually more healthful than their rural hinterlands and are almost as healthful as cities in the most advanced countries. They have participated disproportionately in the miraculous fall in mortality that has occurred in non-industrial countries since 1940—a fall that has enabled them to make death-control gains in twenty years that industrial countries,

Table 4

Population (millions) residing in big cities (500,000 +) in the world and three selected regions, 1920–60

	1920	1930	1940	1950	1960	Increase, 1920–60	Per Cent Increase, 1920–60
World Total	106·6	143·3	181·1	228·2	353·6	247·0	231
Europe	51·7	62·4	68·4	71·3	82·8	31·1	60
Other more developed regions*	41·2	60·3	77·3	101·5	140·2	99·0	241
Third World Countries	13·7	20·6	35·4	55·4	130·6	116·9	836

* Includes Japan, North America, Soviet Union, Temperate South America, Australia, and New Zealand.

SOURCE: United Nations, *Growth of the World's Urban and Rural Population, 1920–2000* (New York, United Nations, 1969).

Table 5

Indicators of living conditions. Countries grouped by national income per capita, post-World War II years

	GROUPS OF COUNTRIES BY PER CAPITA INCOME (U.S. $)					
	1000 and over	575– 1000	350– 575	200– 350	100– 200	Under 100
Urbanisation						
Per cent of total population in urban areas (recent census)	68·2	65·8	49·9	36·0	32·0	22·9
Per cent of population in communities of more than 100,000, about 1955	43	39	35	26	14	9
Mortality						
Expectation of life at birth, 1955–8 (years)	70·6	67·7	65·4	57·4	50·0	41·7
Infant mortality per 1000, 1955–8	24·9	41·9	56·8	97·2	131·1	180·0
Food Consumption						
Per cent of private consumption expenditures spent on food, 1960 or late 1950s (36 countries)	26·2	30·5	36·1	37·6	45·8	55·0
Per capita calorie consumption latest year (40 countries)	3153	2944	2920	2510	2240	2070
Per cent of starchy staples in total calories, latest year (40 countries)	45	53	60	70	74	77
Energy Consumption						
Per capita kilos of coal equivalent, 1956–8	3900	2710	1861	536	265	114
Education						
Per cent of population illiterate, 15 years and over, 1950	2	6	19	30	49	71
Per cent of school enrolment to four-fifths of the 5–19 age group, latest year	91	84	75	60	48	37

starting at a similar level, required 70 to 80 years to achieve. The cities have been the main recipients of this new death control because they are the places to which the medical and scientific techniques, expert personnel, and funds from the advanced nations are first imported and where the most people are reached at least cost.

Nor do conditions in cities of non-industrial countries seem as hostile to reproduction as those of the nineteenth and early twentieth centuries were. Urban fertility remains lower than rural fertility, but not much lower; and in both cases net reproduction rates are higher than they ever were in most of the industrial countries. To some extent this city fertility is a function of good health and low mortality, but it is also a function of some of the very changes that make better health possible. Economic improvement, public welfare, international aid, subsidised housing, and free education make the penalties for having children less than they once were. Giving priority in housing to larger families, maintaining maternal and child health clinics, and discouraging labour-force participation by married women, are additional props to urban reproduction. Equally important are old institutional structures with built-in incentives for prolific breeding—structures that persist in the cities because the paternalism of the times treats them as sacred.

For the new urban residents of the burgeoning Third World cities, such improvements as are taking place create a gulf between where they are and where prior Western experience suggests they might aspire to be—a revolution of rising expectations. As a result, pressures for rapid social change are greater than they were in the West. Lacking an effective capacity to respond, national governments are increasingly confronted by people seeking more revolutionary solutions.

The political circumstances conducive to revolutionary takeovers are there as a result of the recent colonial or neo-colonial status of most of the Third World nations. The imprint of colonialism was, first, that many of the major cities originated as administrative centres for the colonising nations. The recency of independence from colonialism means that most of the developed countries have inherited an intentionally centralised administration, with the result that government involvement is more likely in urban development in the Third World countries today than in the west. In nineteenth-century Europe it was the craftsman and small entrepreneur who promoted industrial development, not the university-educated national bureaucrat. Lacking private development capital and an entrepreneurial class, more Third World development is governmental, involving foreign economic and technical assistance, requiring an assertive governmental role in international diplomacy. As a consequence of governmental leadership in the development process, public goals have priority over private goals.

The colonial powers did not permit effective indigenous leadership to develop. Although the collection, bulking and exporting of industrial raw material required a high degree of organisational and business skills, the logic of the colonial relation was such that the opportunities for doing this were jealously guarded and restricted to citizens of the metropolitan country. Instead, much post-independence leadership developed within the framework of nationalist or revolutionary movements oriented to independent self-determination, albeit on the foundations of western educational experiences, and often with the western model of nineteenth-century urbanisation in mind.

The change in the colonial world came at the end of the Second World War. Initially, the metropolitan powers relinquished controls to parliamentary governments they had created, and to the westernised bureaucratic elites who had served them. In but few cases has parliamentary democracy worked. Most ex-colonial states have moved very quickly to single-party government and to substantially authoritarian control by either the revolutionary elites, who set modernisation as their task, generally with an underlying socialist ideology that leads them to try to create basic structural changes in society and to change the entire social context within which urbanisation is proceeding, or by military juntas whose perspective leads them to seek national efficiency without social change.

The continuing problem resulting from these circumstances is that the cities are becoming the main centres of the social and political changes the new political elites are attempting to produce. This new centrality is a force that attracts people to the cities. The cities have become symbols, drawing in massive immigrant streams, especially of young men, from overcrowded rural areas, only to find rural poverty replaced by urban poverty. To be sure, economic development has the highest national priority in the new governments, but it has failed to keep pace with the growth of urban populations.

In all of these complex changes three themes stand out as revealing most about Third World urbanisation and its human consequences : the nature of migration and the role of peripheral settlements in aiding in the transformation of rural into urban societies—indeed, some say that the city of the future is now emerging in these peripheral settlements; problems associated with absorption of labour into the urban economies, with attendant effects upon the spatial diffusion of growth, upon class structures and class conflict, and upon the integration of developing subcultural mosaics; and the efforts of Third World governments to control the pace, scale and direction of urbanisation, initially with 'western' concepts and ideology as a base, and now by more radical means. These themes will be the focus of what follows in this chapter. The conclusion we reach is that Third World urbanisation is a fundamentally different process than that described by Adna Weber, with human consequences that do not conform to the conventional wisdom codified by Louis Wirth.

MIGRATION AND THE GROWTH OF PERIPHERAL
URBAN SETTLEMENTS

Two demographic factors are of fundamental importance in Third World urbanisation. First is an elevated natural growth rate due to the fact that birth rates have remained almost stable for several decades while death rates have been in decline. Second is the heavy migration from rural areas and more traditional country towns and cities to the principal urban centres of each country, especially to peripheral settlements located in and around the national capitals and regional industrial centres. The impact of internal migration on urbanisation varies according to country and region, but in most cases exceeds fifty per cent of the total population increase, as Table 6 reveals.

The Consequences of Migration
Enough research has now been done on migration in the Third World countries to challenge the socio-political propositions about its consequences inherited from the theorists who codified the nineteenth-century experience in the West. Much of the migration research in the Third World began with borrowed propositions, but increasingly researchers have been led to question this frame-

work and to suggest drastic revisions of the conventional interpretations of the role of the peripheral settlements in the urbanisation process.

Table 6

*Estimates of migrants as a percentage of recent
population increases*

City	Period	Total Population Increase (thousands)	Migrants as a Percentage of Total Population Increase
Abidjan	1955–63	129	76
Bombay	1951–61	1207	52
Caracas	1950–60	587	54
	1960–6	501	50
Djakarta	1961–8	1528	59
Istanbul	1950–60	672	68
	1960–5	428	65
Lagos	1952–62	393	75
Nairobi	1961–9	162	50
São Paulo	1950–60	2163	72
	1960–7	2543	68
Seoul	1955–65	1697	63

SOURCE: World Bank, *Urbanization Sector Working Paper* (Washington,
D.C., The World Bank, June 1972), p. 80.

The borrowed propositions centre on three themes, according to
W. A. Cornelius Jr (1972): material deprivation and frustration
of mobility expectations; personal and social disorganisation; and
political radicalisation and disruptive behaviour. Migrants are
expected to experience the first two conditions and graduate into
the third. Continuing driving forces are held to be the high rates
and volumes of immigration and the limited absorption capacity
of the cities caused by the discrepancy between urban and industrial growth rates. Such theory is distinctively Wirthian, with
roots in Durkheim and Simmel, as well as in the works of Karl
Marx.

But migration research completed in the 1960s provides
startlingly contradictory evidence. Migration, it has been found,
does not necessarily result in severe frustration of expectations for

socio-economic improvement or widespread personal and social disorganisation, and even when these latter conditions are present, they do not necessarily lead to political alienation. Nor does alienation apparently lead to political radicalisation or disruptive behaviour. The urban migrants fail in most respects to conform to the usual conception of a highly politicised, disposable mass. Residents of peripheral settlements rather frequently acquiesce to regimes that sustain the status quo. The dominant perception of the migrants is one of improved living conditions and life chances experienced as a result of the migration to the cities, as well as a fundamental belief in the potential for future betterment and a low tolerance for political risks. Rather than the masses participating in political violence, this has tended to be restricted to student and military elites.

Why is conventional migration theory so deficient? It is now apparent that Wirth's concept of urbanism as a way of life was both time- and culture-bound to the immigrant city of North America in the late nineteenth century. Moreover, it was strongly coloured by a retrospectively idealised conception of the people of 'folk societies' as socially cohesive, personally contented, non-conflictual and well-adjusted, leading to the assertion that urbanisation destroyed this idyllic folk culture.

The limitation of this conventional wisdom is its conceptualisation of urban migrants as an undifferentiated mass responding in uniform fashion to a given set of conditions to which all migrants to large cities are presumably exposed. In reality, migrants comprise a large and disparate array of social types both before and after migration. Distinct migrant subcultures have developed with widely varying life styles, value orientations and levels of subjective political competence. Moreover, a rural–urban dichotomy does not exist; instead there is a broad range of continuity of rural traditions within these urban subcultures (Redfield, 1941 et seq.). Institutions, values and behaviour patterns have persisted or have been adapted to the specific requirements of the urban setting. Social organisation and mutual aid networks continue to function in the urban scene.

Africanists, for example, have described the rise of tribal consciousness in the new African metropolises (Little, 1965; Miner, 1967). This is probably due to conflict with other groups which, as social psychologists have long known, strengthens the internal ties of the collectivity. Most of these studies report that rapid migration has not produced the alienation, anomie, psychological maladjustments and other symptoms of disorganisation held in the Wirthian model to be hallmarks of rapid urbanisation. This is not to say there is no poverty, unemployment, crime and prostitution; these exist in abundance. But for the vast majority of African migrants the ties of the extended family and those between city and village have been maintained. Far from a 'detribalising' process, much of the rich associational life of African cities is based upon common interests, mutual aid, and the need for fellowship of people in the towns who are members of the same tribe or ethnic group, speak the same language, or have come from the same region. Much the same conclusions have been reached in Islamic and Asian urban studies and in investigations of Indian migration to the cities in Latin America. In all cases, ethnic competition remains high and racial confrontation frequent.

Squatter Settlements: The 'Culture of Poverty' Rejected

Most Third World urban growth is concentrated in the so-called 'squatter' or 'uncontrolled' peripheral settlements, which account for a substantial share of city populations throughout the Third World (Table 7). The names vary: in Latin America they are *barrios, barriadas, favelas, ranchos, colonias proletarias*, or *callampas*; in North Africa *bidonvilles* or *gourbivilles*; in India, *bustees*; in Turkey, *gecekondu* districts; in Malaya, *kampongs*; and in the Philippines, *barung-barongs*. The inherited conventional wisdom leads to an interpretation of such settlements as physically decrepit slums, lacking in basic amenities, chaotic, and disorganised—an attitude that persists in much of the urban planning community, which tends to interpret such settlements as obstacles to good civic design.

To cite one example, Morris Juppenlatz (1970), a former UN official, describes them as a 'spreading malady', 'fungus' or 'plague' of 'excessive squalor, filth and poverty . . . human depravity, deprivation, illiteracy, epidemics and sickness' with

growing crime rates and juvenile delinquency . . . land grabbing and disrespect for property rights by a growing number of squatters . . . in the mounting social disorder and tension in the cities, in the weakening and breaking down of the administrative discipline of the authorities, in the unsightly human depravity in the midst of the affluent established urban society, and in the in-

Table 7

Extent of uncontrolled peripheral settlements

Country	City	Year	City Population (thousands)	UNCONTROLLED SETTLEMENT Total (thousands)	UNCONTROLLED SETTLEMENT As percentage of City Population
Africa					
Senegal	Dakar	1969	500	150	30
Tanzania	Dar es Salaam	1967	273	98	36
Zambia	Lusaka	1967	194	53	27
Asia					
China (Taiwan)	Taipei	1966	1300	325	25
India	Calcutta	1961	6700	2220	33
Indonesia	Djakarta	1961	2906	725	25
Iraq	Baghdad	1965	1745	500	29
Malaysia	Kuala Lumpur	1961	400	100	25
Pakistan	Karachi	1964	2280	752	33
Republic of Korea	Seoul	1970	440 (d.u.)*	137 (d.u.)*	30
Singapore	Singapore	1966	1870	980	15
Europe					
Turkey	Total Urban Population	1965	10,800	2365	22
	Ankara	1965	979	460	47
		1970	1250	750	60
	Izmir	1970	640	416	65
North and South America					
Brazil	Rio de Janeiro	1947	2050	400	20
		1957	2940	650	22
		1961	3326	900	27
	Brasilia	1962	148	60	41
Chile	Santiago	1964	2184	546	25
Colombia	Cali	1964	813	243	30
	Buenaventura	1964	111	88	80
Mexico	Mexico City	1952	2372	330	14
		1966	3287	1500	46
Peru	Lima	1957	1261	114	9
		1961	1716	360	21
		1969	2800	1000	36
Venezuela	Caracas	1961	1330	280	21
		1964	1590	556	35
	Maracaibo	1966	559	280	50

* Dwelling units.

SOURCE: U.N. General Assembly, *Housing, Building and Planning: Problems and Priorities in Human Settlements*, Report of the Secretary-General, August 1970, Annex III, p. 55. Definitions vary. Additional details are given in the source quoted.

adequacy of the essential public services . . . As the political control of the cities . . . passes from the presently established urban society . . . into the hands of the emergent urban squatter society who have little or no heritage of city-dwelling . . . it can be expected that essential services will diminish until they finally break down and collapse.

Such views have been given apparent intellectual support by scholars like the American anthropologist Oscar Lewis, who, in his research in the 1950s and 1960s described a subculture with a life style that he felt transcended national boundaries and regional and rural–urban differences within nations. This subculture he called the *culture of poverty*, of the slum, the ghetto, the squatter settlement. Wherever it occurs, Lewis argued, its practitioners exhibit remarkable similarity in the structure of their families, in interpersonal relations, in spending habits, in their value systems and in their orientation in time.

His studies identified a large number of traits that characterise the culture of poverty. The principal ones may be described along four dimensions of the system : the relationship between the subculture and the larger society; the nature of the 'ghetto' community; the nature of the family; and the attitudes, values and character structure of the individual.

The disengagement, the non-integration, of the poor with respect to the major institutions of society Lewis felt to be a crucial element in the culture of poverty. It reflects the combined effect of a variety of factors including poverty, to begin with, but also segregation and discrimination, fear, suspicion and apathy and the development of alternative institutions and procedures in the slum community. The people do not belong to labour unions or political parties and make little use of banks, hospitals, department stores or museums. Such involvement as there is in the institutions of the larger society—in the jails, the army and the public welfare system—does little to suppress the traits of the culture of poverty.

People in a culture of poverty, Lewis argued, produce little wealth and receive little in return. Chronic unemployment and underemployment, low wages, lack of property, lack of savings, absence of food reserves in the home and chronic shortage of cash imprison the family and the individual in a vicious circle. Thus, for lack of cash, the slum house-holder makes frequent purchases of small quantities of food at higher prices. The slum economy turns inward; it shows a high incidence of pawning of personal goods, borrowing at usurious rates of interest, informal credit arrangements among neighbours, use of secondhand clothing and furniture.

There is awareness of middle-class values. People talk about them and even claim some of them as their own. On the whole, however, they do not live by them. They will declare that marriage by the law, by the church or by both is the ideal form of marriage, but few will marry. For men who have no steady jobs, no property and no prospect of wealth to pass on to their children, who live in the present without expectations of the future, who want to avoid the expense and legal difficulties involved in marriage and divorce, a free union or consensual marriage makes good sense. The women, for their part, will turn down offers of marriage from men who are likely to be immature and generally unreliable. They feel that a consensual union gives them some of the freedom and flexibility men have. By not giving the fathers of their children legal status as husbands, the women have a stronger claim on the children. They also maintain exclusive rights to their own property.

Along with the disengagement from the larger society, Lewis felt there to be a hostility to the basic institutions of what are regarded as the dominant classes : hatred of police, mistrust of government and of those in high positions and a cynicism that extends to the church. The culture of poverty thus, he felt, holds a certain potential for protest and for entrainment in political movements aimed against the existing order.

With its poor housing and overcrowding, the community of the culture of poverty is high in gregariousness, but Lewis argued that it has a minimum of organisation beyond the nuclear and extended family. Occasionally slum-dwellers come together in temporary informal groupings; neighbourhood gangs that cut across slum settlements represent a considerable advance beyond the zero point of the continuum. It is the low level of organisation that gives the culture of poverty its marginal and anomalous quality.

The family in the culture of poverty, according to Lewis, does not cherish childhood as a specially prolonged and protected stage in the life cycle. Initiation into sex comes early. With the instability of consensual marriage the family tends to be mother-centred and tied more closely to the mother's extended family.

The female head of the house is given to authoritarian rule. In spite of much verbal emphasis on family solidarity, sibling rivalry for the limited supply of goods and maternal affection is intense. There is little privacy.

The individual who grows up in this culture has a strong feeling of fatalism, helplessness, dependence and inferiority. These traits, so often remarked in the current literature as characteristic of the American Negro, Lewis felt to be equally strong in slum-dwellers elsewhere in the world who are not segregated or discriminated against as a distinct ethnic or racial group. Other traits include a high incidence of weak ego structure, orality and confusion of sexual identification, all reflecting maternal deprivation; a strong present-time orientation with relatively little disposition to defer gratification and plan for the future; and a high tolerance for psychological pathology of all kinds. There is a widespread belief in male superiority and among the men a strong preoccupation with machismo, their masculinity.

Lewis felt that these people, provincial and local in outlook, with little sense of history, know only their own neighbourhood and their own way of life. Usually they do not have the knowledge, the vision or the ideology to see the similarities between their troubles and those of their counterparts elsewhere in the world. And he concluded that they are not class-conscious, although they are sensitive indeed to symbols of status.

Lewis has been criticised by his peers (Valentine, 1968; Leacock, 1971), and what is emerging throughout the world is an alternative interpretation : *that under conditions of rapid urbanisation the uncontrolled new settlements play an important functional role.* William Mangin (1967) has written that squatter settlements represent a *solution* to the complex problem of urbanisation and migration, combined with a housing shortage. While there are indeed some 'slums of despair' displaying the traits listed by Lewis in *both* advanced and Third World countries, many studies have shown that so-called squatter settlements vary widely in their properties. Clinard (1966) writes that although some squatter settlements show disorganisation, it is important that each be examined in the light of its own distinctive subculture, which is the dominant influence on the life pattern of its inhabitants. Of critical significance is how the settlement was formed, e.g. by organised squatter invasion, gradual accretion, or government initiation, and whether or not there is a sense of ownership or control of property.

John Turner has distinguished three different economic levels of the transitional urban settlements :

1. *The low-income bridgeheads.* Populated by recent arrivals to the city, with few marketable skills, the need to obtain and hold work dominates. Modern standards have low priority, and access is all important. Thus, such bridgeheads tend to be in decaying old homes in the central city, or in the centrally located 'slums of despair'. They are poor, and lack essential services.

2. *The low-income consolidators.* As stability of a permanent income is achieved, access is no longer so critical (often because public transport is cheap), although conventional housing is still out of reach. Money is available for other than necessities, and family orientation begins to dominate in more peripheral squatter 'slums of hope'. Many such settlements are highly organized and planned, and upgrade in quality through self-help efforts over the years, providing shelter and security without imposing on the residents the middle-class's priorities for housing.

3. *The middle-income status seekers.* Those with economic security then seek social status through choice of location—in Rio de Janeiro, this was adjacent to the high-status 'conventional' residential areas. Upgrading of housing quality assumes priority, along with education and quality of services.

Thus, no universal form of decaying slum settlement is to be found, but instead a range of markedly different settlement types with fundamentally different subcultures. As Robert J. Crooks, Director of the United Nations Centre for Housing, Building and Planning comments, they are better called *transitional urban settlements*, which he feels demonstrate remarkable vigour and ingenuity in improving their living conditions.

One of the most important variables confounding conventional western wisdom about the experience of the new migrant in the transitional settlements that has been pointed out is the role of traditional networks of social relations, which have facilitated successful assimilation of many migrants into urban life. In Africa, as we noted earlier, these networks involve a continuity of rural ways in the city and E. M. Bruner has shown in a study of northern Sumatra that

the cultural premises and roots of urban Batak life are to be found in village society . . . Most urban Batak have more meaningful associations with their rural residents in the highlands than with their non-Batak neighbours.

Similarly, Janet Abu-Lughod concluded in studies of Cairo that the Wirthian model of anonymity, secondary contacts and anomie does not obtain. L. Alan Eyre has described the 'shantytown' resident of Montego Bay as 'the poor suburbanite of the developing world . . . upwardly mobile . . . industrious . . . a saver . . . more often a conservative than a radical'.

Even Calcutta's teeming *bustees* have been described by Colin Rosser as performing six functions which are of major importance to the urbanisation process as a whole. They provide housing at rents that are within the means of the lowest income groups. They act as reception centres for migrants, providing a mechanism to assist in adaptation to urban life. They provide within the *bustee* a wide variety of employment in marginal and small-scale enterprises. They provide a means of finding accommodation in close proximity to work. Their social and communal organisation provides essential social support in unemployment and other occasions of difficulty. Finally, they encourage and reward small-scale private entrepreneurship in the field of housing.

But the conventional wisdom still dominates attitudes of many policy-makers, stereotyping all transitional settlements as social aberrations, 'cancers' overwhelming an otherwise healthy municipal body. In many cases, governments have responded by the expulsion of squatters and the costly and disruptive clearance of slum areas, resulting in a net reduction of housing available to low income groups, as when, in 1963, inner-city Manila squatters were relocated to an unprepared site deep in the countryside at Sapaney Palay, or more recently, as the Brazilian government has eliminated the *favelas* from Rio de Janeiro. Where clearance together with rehousing has been attempted, it has generally resulted in the unproductive use of scarce public resources, meagre improvements if any, and unequal treatment of the families inhabiting transitional areas.

This is because public housing programmes frequently attempt to follow the pattern set in the more developed countries. Complete dwellings are constructed prior to occupancy, at minimum space and material standards. But even these standards tend to be too costly in relation to total needs and total resources available. Rarely are they a realistic solution for most squatters and slum-dwellers, as they involve heavy interest and maintenance costs, apart from the high capital costs per family. If rents are high enough to amortise investments, they are likely to be far above the ability of the people to pay, creating a high rate of default. However, the most serious criticism of pre-built housing projects is that financially they remain beyond the grasp of precisely the group most in need of housing assistance, those with the lowest incomes occupying transitional settlement areas. One of the few successful examples of resettlement via low-cost building programmes may be in Singapore, where the Housing and Development Board created in 1960 has tackled the problem with all the energy of the welfare socialism of that city-state's government.

Because of the self-improving nature of the transitional settlements, the United Nations Centre for Housing, Building and Planning now stresses the importance of achieving a major shift in attitude and emphasis from the current norms of national and international policies and programmes which attempt to deal with transitional urban settlements. The most basic policy and programme directions are the acceptance and support of the long-term existence of transitional areas and adequate pre-planning for future transitional settlement growth. The Centre notes that in many cases, transitional urban settlements constitute valuable actual or potential additions to the urban housing stock and fixed capital investment at city and national scales. In conditions of rapid urbanisation and even more rapid growth of transitional areas, through migration and natural population growth, vast clearance schemes, with or without high-cost public housing, can only aggravate the problems of people living in these areas. It therefore recommends that, consistent with a positive supportive attitude, governments should take action to make normal urban utilities and community services available to these areas, according to priorities established through the involvement of the residents themselves in the development process. Because of the importance of the degree to which the residents feel a secure right to the land they occupy, the Centre recommends that supportive programmes should treat this issue as a matter of high priority. And because the forces leading to the rapid growth of transitional urban settlements will continue, they recommend pre-planning for transitional settlement growth, in a manner that will emphasise the positive aspects of these areas. They note that clearance of slum and squatter areas is a waste of popular resource investment and often results in a net destruction of the living environment. Governments and international organisations, they say, must develop and use legal and administrative mechanisms which will make possible planned land acquisition and development in urban areas in advance of need, taking into account not only the possibility of extending utilities and community facilities to the areas, but also other key aspects such as transportation and location in relation to jobs.

ABSORPTION OF LABOUR IN THE URBAN ECONOMY

The most pressing problems associated with Third World urbanisation arise because, despite accelerated industrialisation, the rapidly increasing labour force of the cities is not being absorbed into full and productive employment (Friedmann and Sullivan, 1972). With urban growth rates typically running at least twice the rate of natural increase, frequently in excess of 5·0 per cent per annum (Davis, 1969), but with industrial employment increasing at 4·4 per cent per annum (Turnham and Jaeger, 1971), the bulk of new manpower is absorbed by small-scale enterprise, personal services and open unemployment. Moreover, spurts in urban investment tend only to bring more migrants to the city. Several consequences flow from these facts: maintenance of a minimal 'survival economy'; the reinforcement of traditional subcultures in the city; the prevention of diffusion of development beyond the big cities and the creation, thereby, of growing primacy of the major urban agglomerations.

Structure of the Urban Economies

These consequences may be understood in terms of the structure of the urban economies, which are made up of three separate sectors. The *individual enterprise* sector comprises the unemployed workers of the 'street economy' of the city, including the offspring of urban residents, recent migrants to the city, those laid off from other jobs, street hawkers, casual construction workers, prostitutes and panderers, professional beggars and petty thieves. It accounts for between 25 and 40 per cent of the urban labour force. Few earn more than the subsistence minimum, and those who do most frequently share the surplus with their kin. There is intense competition for work and this keeps earnings at the subsistence minimum. Any growth in the urban economy simply

brings in more migrants and keeps rewards to individual enterprise at the lowest possible level. Most people engaged in this
sector live marginal lives in the bridgehead settlements, or simply
live on the streets, and under the worst conditions experience
large scale misery in its full harshness. At night the sidewalks of
Calcutta, for example, become public dormitories, heaped with
emaciated men, women, old people and children. The poor of Calcutta lack the most elementary belongings, owning neither pillow,
mattress nor blanket; their bodies stink and are covered by soiled
rags. At dawn, before the city awakens, carts collect the corpses
of those who have died in the night.

The second sector of the Third World's urban economies is that
devoted to *family enterprise* in the traditional bazaar-type economies. The land use patterns of the parts of the city in which this
sector dominates are chaotic. Such family enterprise accounts for
35–45 per cent of the labour force in small trade and service
establishments and industrial workshops. By and large, traditional
commodities are produced for the low-income mass market using
local raw materials and lacking quality control and standardisation. Production is dependent on the utilisation of the entrepreneur's family (the extended kin group), for whom the end-product
is a condition of shared poverty. Because pricing is competitive
and the activities are labour-intensive, returns seldom provide for
more than the subsistence requirements of the family.

The third sector is the *corporate*, including capital-intensive
businesses, the government, and the professions. Depending upon
the particular city and country, this sector provides between 15
and 50 per cent of the urban employment. Economic units are
larger, people work regular hours, capital investment is on a large
scale, levels of technology and productivity are high. There is
continuing pressure to provide all the perquisites of similar occupations in the developed countries. Education is required for
entry to the sector, and employment in it automatically conveys
middle-class status as a minimum, and produces the professional-
managerial urban elite at its upper echelons, together with the
juxtaposition of luxury and poverty that is one of the striking physical characteristics of the Third World cities.

This structure of the urban economy is argued by T. G. McGee
(1967) to be a direct product of the colonial or neo-colonial experience of most Third World countries. Early European contact

saw the establishment of embryonic colonial urban networks designed largely to aid European control of indigenous trade. Western controls expanded in the nineteenth century, involving creation of far more extensive urban and communications networks
than had existed in the area before. But the colonial city remained
essentially a conservative force, economically subordinate to the
metropolis and world trade. The culture, way of life and population of the city were alien to the indigenous inhabitants, for the
cities were populated by heterogeneous populations, many of
whom were migrants or foreigners. Occupational and residential
segregation existed according to ethnic groups, as did social stratification; Europeans at the top, commercial groups (frequently
Asiatic) in the middle with the local Western-educated elites, and
finally the indigenous immigrant population at the bottom. Much
of the indigenous population was transitory, young and male.
Even today, McGee argues, with inherited colonial economic
structures displaying excessive specialisation in the production of
raw materials for the industries of the metropolitan powers, major
cities of the Third World still tend to function as 'head-links'
between the industrialised powers and their sources of raw
materials. In a sense, then, they remain transplants more closely
related to the industrial world than to the countryside of the Third
World.

There are, of course, differences from one type of city to another. McGee reports that the 'metropoles' of Southeast Asia, as
elsewhere in the Third World, have clearly become part of a
new worldwide urban 'super-culture'. They are connecting links
with other nations and integrating centres of economic, political
and intellectual life. Beyond these metropolises, in the provincial
towns, life remains traditional, however, revolving around two
main institutional complexes, government and trade. The trans-
mission of ideas to and by those provincial towns is quite limited
because socio-political structures tend to be authoritarian, hierarchical, and centralised.

Maintenance of the Survival Economy

A particular set of labour market dynamics between the three sectors maintains workers in the urban economy at base survival
levels. Any growth in the corporate or family enterprise sectors,

for example, filters immediately to the individual enterprise sector. The prospect of gaining employment brings more new migrants into the city and intense competition for jobs keeps wage rates at their minimum. To add to the downward pressure on wages, expansion of mass production by the corporate sector frequently forces family sector enterprises producing inferior goods out of business. The higher productivity of the corporate sector means that job gains are less than production gains, while job losses in the family sector are substantial. The consequences may be seen in both social class terms and in terms of urban primacy.

Reinforcement of Traditional Subcultures

Shared poverty is therefore the rule for the majority in the Third World cities. One major result is to reaffirm the critical importance of maintaining the mutual aid networks that honour traditional family and tribal obligations and produce increasing rivalries among tribal and ethnic groups and social classes.

The social structure of the Third World's cities has at its apex today the westernised elite, the reference group for the aspiring masses. Beneath is an ethnically heterogeneous population in which, out of competition for jobs, ethnic rivalries have become more pronounced and 'tribalism' has increased. Many of the alien middlemen groups have been or are rapidly being eliminated. Out of this new social stratification have arisen new forms of class conflict. On the one hand, there are pressures for social ascent in the new elite based upon superior education and individual achievement in the occupational and professional world. On the other hand, continued links to less-advantaged kinsmen produce sharing based upon reciprocity and the mutual benefit flowing from such relationships, leading to maintenance of rural ways in the city (Marris, 1967). The new class conflict comes between the two—between occupational achievement and kin-group relations when reciprocity can no longer be maintained by the less advantaged. Such conflicts must be seen in a situation in which aspirations have risen far more rapidly than absolute gains in welfare. Politicians, drawn from the new elite, have tended to portray the benefits of independence in far more glowing terms than have been realised, leading to conflicts over wage demands by urban workers, and growing socialist pressures for reducing the privileges of the elite and creating classless societies. The counter-thrust has been a series of military coups and the present authoritarian systems of government.

Diffusion and Primacy

Maintenance of wages at survival levels by the flows of migrant labour into the individual enterprise sector in response to perceived employment opportunities has consequences beyond those already discussed. To understand these it is first necessary to understand certain features of the urban growth process in the developed countries, where different labour market conditions obtain.

Let us take the United States as an example (an identical argument applies to western Europe versus the overseas colonies and dominions). As the process of industrial urbanisation ran its course, the north-eastern manufacturing belt became the central driving force of the economy in the later nineteenth century, a great heartland nucleation of industry and the national market, the focus of large-scale national-serving industry, the seedbed of new industry responding to the dynamic structure of national final demand, and the centre of high levels of per capita income. This core region became the lever for development of more peripheral hinterland regions, both in North America and beyond, reaching out to them for their resources as its input requirements increased, stimulating their growth in accordance with its resource demands and the resource endowment of the regions. Thus, standing in a dependent relationship to the heartland, radiating out across the national landscape, there developed resource-dominant regional hinterlands specialising in the production of resource and intermediate outputs for which the heartland reached out to satisfy the input requirements of its great manufacturing plants. In the hinterlands, resource-endowment became a critical determinant of the particular cumulative advantage of the region and hence its growth potential.

The result of such core-centred patterns of growth was thus a high degree of regional specialisation. Specialisation, in turn, determined the content and direction of regional growth. Regional economic growth in every case became externally determined by national demands for regional specialties. The nature of these specialties, alternative sources of them, and changes in the structure of demand therefore determined in large measure the nature and extent of regional growth. This extended to the secondary support needed by export industries—housing, public facilities, retail establishments, service facilities and the like.

Emerging systems of cities played a critical role in the whole process, for cities became the instruments whereby the specialised sub-regions were reticulated in national economies. They became the centres of activity and of innovation, focal points of transport networks, locations of superior accessibility at which firms could most easily reap scale economies of localisation and urbanisation. Agricultural enterprise became more efficient in the vicinity of cities. The more prosperous commercialised agricultures encircled the major cities, whereas the inaccessible peripheries of the great urban regions were characterised by backward, subsistence economic systems.

This spatial organisation involved two major elements : *systems of cities*, arranged in hierarchies according to the functions performed by each; and corresponding areas of urban influence or *urban fields* surrounding each of the cities in these systems. Generally, the size and functions of a city and the extent of its urban field developed proportionally. Each major region developed around a centre of metropolitan rank, and the network of inter-metropolitan connections emerged as the mesh reticulating a whole set of such regions. The spatial incidence of economic growth became a function of distance from the metropolises. Troughs of economic backwardness hung on in the most inaccessible areas along the intermetropolitan peripheries. Further sub-regional articulation was provided by successively smaller centres at progressively lower levels of the hierarchy—smaller cities, towns, villages, etc.—and as transportation was improved, the lowest level centres, after initially important roles, began to wither and vanish.

In such circumstances, impulses of economic and social change moved along three planes : outwards from heartland metropolises to those of the regional hinterlands in a national-level 'spread effect'; from centres of higher to centres of lower level in the hierarchy in a pattern of 'hierarchical diffusion'; and outward from urban centres into their surrounding urban fields in a hinterland spread pattern. Part of this diffusion mechanism has been found in the operation of urban labour markets. When growth was sustained over long periods, economic expansion in high-income areas and the heartland metropolises produced labour shortages and a rising wage-rate. Labour-intensive industries, therefore, were priced out of the high-income labour markets and shifted to smaller urban centres and more peripheral areas. The significance of this 'filtering' or 'trickle-down' process lay not only in its direct but also in its indirect effects. The induced effects on real income and employment were frequently considerable in the low-income regions because prices there tended to rise less and because capital substitution led to output per worker becoming greater. Where the boom was maintained, industries of higher labour productivity shifted into lower-income areas, and the lower-wage industries were forced to move into even smaller towns and more isolated areas.

If such processes operate over a long period of time, they produce and maintain an urban system comprising a few large metropolises, a larger number of intermediate size cities, and a still larger number of smaller towns, all sharing in the national growth process and distributing its benefits throughout both heartland and hinterland regions.

Such a 'balanced' system of cities has been described as producing a 'rank-size distribution' of cities (Berry, 1971). As defined by G. K. Zipf, who first identified it, a rank-size distribution arises if, when cities are ranked in decreasing order of size and plotted in a graph prepared on doubly-logarithmic paper with population on one axis and rank on the other, the plot forms a straight line. Zipf thought that such straight-line relationships reflected the achievement of national unity in both political and economic terms.

Where the population of the largest city exceeds the figure that might be expected on the basis of the rank-size distribution, a condition of 'primacy' is said to exist. Colin Clark (1967) uses the additional term 'oligarchy' to describe situations in which the towns over 100,000 population have a bigger share of the total urban population than would be expected from the straight-line relationship, but where, at the same time, the primacy of the leading city is kept in check. A particularly striking example is provided by the Portuguese colonial system, in which the major urban 'head-links' form one oligarchic rank-size regime and centres functioning at the local levels of the hierarchy form another (Fig. 11).

The idea of primacy was initially formulated by Mark Jefferson

(1938), and was very simple. He argued that everywhere 'nationalism crystallises in primate cities . . . supereminent . . . not merely in size, but in national influence'. He assessed the degree of eminence of cities within countries by computing the ratios of size of the second- and third-ranking cities to that of the largest place. But immediately after Jefferson's papers had appeared, Zipf directed attention to the entire system of cities. The rank-size distribution, he argued, was the situation to be expected in any 'homogeneous socio-economic system' that had reached a state of 'harmonious equilibrium'.

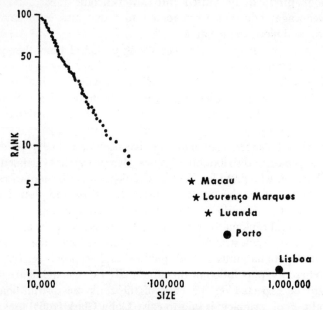

FIG. 11   Rank-size relationship for cities of the Portuguese colonial system

The latest census data are used.

It remained for discussants at a series of post-war UNESCO conferences on urbanisation in Asia and the Far East, and in Latin America, to put the two together and to point out the links to Louis Wirth's social doctrines. Cases deviating from the rank-size distribution were said to arise from 'over-urbanisation' of the economies of lesser-developed countries because of 'excessive' in-migration and superimposition of limited economic development of a colonial type, creating 'dual economies' characterised by 'primate cities' that tend to have 'paralytic' effects upon the development of smaller urban places, to be 'parasitic' in relation to the remainder of the national economy, and to be productive of alienation, anomie and social disorganisation.

Obviously, each of the words in quotation marks involves a value judgment, but they do reveal that the idea of the primate city is firmly established in many people's minds as a malignant deviation from expectations about hierarchical organisation derived from the rank-size rule, with obvious pejorative connotations.

In fact, the reasons for primacy are straightforward. Instead of development filtering down the urban hierarchy and spreading its effects outwards within urban fields, growth is concentrated in the major cities. This is because each increment to the urban economy draws in more migrants, to maintain wages at the subsistence minimums, in the manner described earlier. There is no incentive for growth to decentralise. Modern enterprise remains concentrated in the major cities. Modernising influences reach the migrants, but in the hinterlands traditional ways of life remain in the small towns and villages. Increasing primacy is, in turn, a sign that economic growth is taking place and affecting more people.

THE URGE TO PLAN

Yet to many planners and policy-makers in the developing countries, 'gigantism' of the largest cities is still a characteristic to be feared, even when the principal city is small relative to cities in other areas. This fear is manifested in the expressed desire on the part of public officials to gain control over the urbanisation process and to restrict population growth in the primate cities. The reasons given usually are uncontrolled urban sprawl, traffic congestion, unemployment, crime, proliferation of squatters communities, inability to provide services and, in general, a fear that living standards could be depressed by further uncontrolled growth. Also perceived by the western-educated planners are 'diseconomies of scale' and the primate city as a 'parasite'.

The feeling is that continued change within the framework of present economic systems will produce only more and worse problems, and that changes in the nature of urban systems must be produced to overcome the continuing constraints of low rates of economic growth, export orientation and colonial inheritance that conspire to confine modernising influences to primate cities with little foreseeable hope for filtering to take place. The increasing feeling is that experiences of developed nations are irrelevant in the Third World today, and so radical new approaches to planning are being tried.

The developed countries, it is argued, were economically ahead of the rest of the world when they commenced modern economic growth, and the underdeveloped countries are the worst off economically at the present time. The world of the eighteenth and nineteenth centuries had freer trade policies, freer opportunities for international movements of population and less political and economic barriers than the world of today. In the Third World institutional settings which are the products of modern economic growth have preceded the process of growth. The political institution of democracy, for instance, often precludes the exploitation of the proletariat for the purpose of growth, a feature which was not uncommon in the initial stages of growth in the West. Welfare measures like minimum wages, regulation of hours of work, prohibition of child labour, are all institutions which in certain ways do not make for economic development of the sort that took place under early western capitalism. This is compounded by the coexistence of highly developed countries with rapid means of communication and transportation that enables peoples of the underdeveloped countries to copy consumption patterns of the developed countries. This 'demonstration effect' is assymetrical, i.e. it applies to consumption but not to investment and saving patterns, thus diverting resources from investment to conspicuous and other types of consumption. Parallel 'derived development' projects divert investments to conspicuous and monumental structures rather than to productive ones. For all these reasons, Third World planning is trying to produce by other means the 'balanced' urban distributions that 'normal' growth processes will not produce.

Many dramatic new policies are trying, for example, to promote urban decentralisation through investment incentive programmes, growth pole strategies, regional development schemes, and the like. In Indonesia rapid urban growth of a major city has been challenged frontally. The city of Djakarta issues a required residency permit to new in-migrants only upon certification of lodging and employment. The new arrival must deposit with the city government for six months the equivalent of return fare to the point of origin. It is claimed that this policy, initiated in late 1970, has cut migration by as much as 50 per cent. Such asserted successes are now leading other leaders and planners to try to devise equally radical solutions to the perceived urban problems.

Planning is thus the order of the day—national, regional and urban. But in a 1972 survey of urban development efforts in the Third World, the U.S. Agency for International Development reported that most national development plans traditionally have given only token attention to urban development. To the extent that urban considerations have been incorporated, the focus has been primarily on housing and expressed in terms of a housing sector. In some places, for example Singapore and Brazil, substantial gains have been made towards solving housing difficulties through national sectoral planning. Those few instances in which national planning for urban development has gone beyond this narrow approach are conspicuous and groundbreaking. These range from national infrastructural development priorities in Turkey to a plan for all-out restructuring of society through urbanisation and urban development in Malaysia. In the mid-range there are Brazil's long-standing preoccupation with national political, social, and economic integration and Colombia's urban sectoral programme aimed at reducing population flow to major cities and at stimulating development on a regional basis.

Brazil's programmes have never congealed into a national whole; nevertheless, in the past decade they have produced massive separate endeavours, each entrepreneurial in the sense of trying to create growth opportunities, such as transferring the national capital from coastal Rio de Janeiro to the interior at Brasilia, development of well over 100 new towns in the south, promotion of a large-scale growth pole development programme through infrastructure and investment incentives to stimulate development of the north-east and help stem its rapid out-migration, and construction of a trans-Amazonian highway to open up that region and stimulate strategic urban growth centres along the route.

Colombia is attempting a more orchestrated and comprehensive programme nationally, specifically to foster the development of intermediate-sized cities as countermagnets to the major population centres.

Malaysia's programme is outlined comprehensively in its new Five-Year National Development Plan. The Plan places priority on urban development and rural-urban migration as a tool for achieving its goal of restructuring society to meet the larger needs and to bring more Malays into the economic mainstream. It is a dramatic attempt to promote fundamental societal changes quickly. To help co-ordinate and implement the urbanisation features of the new plan, an Urban Development Authority was created in the Office of the Prime Minister. Other units in the Prime Minister's Office also will be actively engaged in plan implementation. Both the overall strategy and the concentration of co-ordinating and implementing authority for urban development at such a high level are unprecedented.

Regional planning and development goals appear as new ingredients in many national development plans (e.g. those of Brazil, Colombia, Chile, Ivory Coast, Morocco, Kenya, Nigeria, Turkey, India, Thailand and Korea), and they are under serious discussion in other countries (such as Panama, Vietnam, Indonesia and Pakistan).

However, in spite of all of this attention and application, regional planning means many things to many people. Much of the action in regional planning and development is tentative and experimental in nature. In a number of countries regional planning has been applied in piecemeal fashion in attempts to encourage development of backward regions, such as north-eastern Brazil and northern Thailand. Similarly, the strong notion of regional development in Turkey is related to a desire to achieve more 'balanced' growth by stimulating development in the south and especially in the east. It includes the idea of trying to develop counter-magnets to the largest cities—that is, to encourage the growth of cities in the 20,000 to 100,000 size class. Incentives such as tax breaks, special amortisation, and exceptions to corporate income laws have been given to industry. Professional salaries have been supplemented and embryonic regional universities begun. In fact, regional planning of this kind preceded the development of the current National Plan in Turkey.

The concept of growth centres and growth poles in regional development is perhaps the most common application of regional planning. The most specific example of this within a national planning framework is Colombia. For planning purposes the country has been split into four major economic regions, each one having one of the four major cities as a growth pole : Barranquilla for Atlantic Coast, Cali in south-west, Medellin in north-west, and Bogotá in central. Kenya too has regional physical development plans incorporating a growth pole concept, and Indonesian planners are grappling with more fundamental aspects of regional planning as it affects the development of cities —namely, defining the functions of economic regions, identifying growth poles within the regions, and assessing the real and potential role of these cities within each region or sub-region (area).

Planning for new towns is part of the growth centre planning process; there are numerous examples in the developing countries. These range from the massive endeavour required to establish the 'new town' new captital of Brazil at interior Brasilia to the creation of the new rural communities in connection with the Bandama River Valley project in Ivory Coast. Somewhere in the mid-range is the new satellite town approach in which new towns are created on the periphery of major urban centres, either as bedroom communities, industrial complexes, or as combined industrial, commercial and residential complexes.

Tax incentives are rapidly gaining in popularity as a related locational tool. Examples can be found in Brazil, Colombia, Turkey, Ivory Coast, Thailand, Indonesia and Malaysia. The tax and infrastructure incentive for commercial location at specific growth points in north-east Brazil is a case in point. It was thought that, by allowing tax exemption on 50 per cent of all profits invested in the north-east, business investments would flow into designated growth centres. The government would encourage development further by creation of physical infrastructure. Because the goal was development of lagging areas presumed to have growth potential, the already burgeoning cities of Salvador and Recife were excluded from the plan; the incentives did not apply in these two cities. It was found, however, that investments did not flow to the designated growth points throughout the region as planned. Instead they tended to cluster at the municipal boundaries of Recife and Salvador. This is testimony to the effectiveness of tax incentives to locational decisions and also to the strong pull effects exerted on industry and commerce by major metropolitan centres.

An alternative approach is under consideration whereby concentric zones of increasing tax incentives would be established around Recife and Salvador. It is hoped that this change will help achieve the objectives of the original policy; namely, the development of the lagging regions contributing so heavily to the chronic out-migration of the north-east.

At a lesser level than regional growth centre planning, but often a component of regional planning, is the area development planning found in Ivory Coast, Kenya, Morocco, Malaysia, Indonesia, and elsewhere. More rural in its orientation, it focuses on specific projects or resettlement areas. The approach is essentially physical, concentrating on infrastructure. Frequently special development authorities or semi-public companies are established to help oversee the planning and development of the area.

An example of such a complex is the Bandama Valley Authority (AVB) in Ivory Coast. Similar to the TVA (Tennessee Valley Authority) in the United States, it was set up to oversee development of a dam, a man-made lake, and related projects which will involve 720 square miles, 100 villages and settlements, and 70,000 people.

The physical plan for the Island (Province) of Bali is an example of area planning on a more comprehensive scale. Because the primary functions of Bali are already clear (namely, tourism and rice culture), the Indonesian government established a centrally assisted area planning unit in Denpasar which might serve as a model for the rest of the country. The physical plan for the island, including urban and rural areas, was completed in 1971.

Planning at the municipal level has long been applied in one form or another in most developing countries. It has taken place within highly centralised national government structures, largely without benefit of national policy guidelines or budgetary priority and frequently under constraint of obsolete laws and codes. The plans usually are regarded with great expectations, usually not realised. Some of the problems with urban planning arise from the physical approach, which has dominated. The professionals tend to be primarily engineers and architects. This approach deals very superficially with the economic, social, legal, environmental, political, and institutional aspects of urban development. It usually fails to encompass the developmental interaction between city and hinterland and the linkages between cities. The approach too often has been narrowly sectoral or project oriented (e.g. a master plan for sewerage, transportation, or a specific housing project) without regard to impact on or relationship to other elements of the urban system. This is true also of most forms of capital investment projects.

Urban planning has a particularly unimpressive record. There seems to be a consensus today in the Third World that traditional master planning, being costly, time consuming, static, and frequently done by expatriates, is not the appropriate approach in a developmental context. Alien solutions abound. Examples are model cities programmes, urban renewal, Western-type urban freeways and circumferential highways, 'City Beautiful' planning approaches, and new towns decentralisation programmes. And the plans proposing these alien solutions are often obsolete before they are ever published. For example, the master plan for Kuala Lumpur was begun in 1965 on the basis of 1964 data. It was completed in 1969 and published in 1970. A master plan for Bangkok was completed 20 years ago and updated 10 years later, but has never been accepted or implemented.

In spite of some of the radical solutions now being proposed that have been listed above, what characterises most of the planning efforts in the Third World is the absence of will to plan effectively, and more often than not, political smokescreening. Most urbanisation policy is unconscious, partial, unco-ordinated and negative (Dotson, 1972). It is unconscious in the sense that those who effect it are largely unaware of its proportions and features. It is partial in that few of the points at which governments might act to manage urbanisation and affect its course and direction are in fact utilised. It is unco-ordinated in that national planning tends to be economic and urban planning tends to be physical, and the disjunction often produces competing policies. It is negative in that the ideological perspective of the planners leads them to try to divert, retard or stop urban growth, and in particular to inhibit the expansion of metropolises and primate cities.

Elsewhere, in Maoist China for example, this anti-urban bias is also clear (Lewis, 1971). In China it has obvious historical roots in the history of the Chinese Communist Party and its struggle for power before 1949 and in the modern history of a China dominated by treaty-port colonialists who controlled and shaped nearly all of its large cities. These cities were also the homes of the

Chinese bourgeoisie. They were felt to have been reactionary in the past, potentially revisionist now and in the future, and alienating at all times. Thus, their growth in China continues to be controlled by an uprecedented policy which limits their size and which channels new industrial investment into new or smaller cities in previously remote or backward areas, or into rural communes, which are to be made industrially as self-sufficient as possible without acquiring the morally corrupting and alienating qualities of big cities, nor their damaging effects on the environment. City-dwellers, especially white collar workers, must spend a month or more every year, whatever their status, in productive physical labour in the countryside, where they may regain 'correct' values. The distinctions between mental and manual labour, city and countryside, 'experts' or bureaucrats and peasants or workers are to be eliminated. The benefits and the experience of industrialisation and modernisation are to be diffused uniformly over the landscape and to all of the people, while the destructive, de-humanising, corrupting aspects of over-concentration in cities are to be avoided.

TWO CASES OF NATIONAL URBAN PLANNING AT THE THIRD WORLD'S MARGINS

The keys to the Maoist reconstruction of China have been a will to plan, clear objectives, and totalitarian powers. There are two other cases in the world where these three prerequisites have combined to produce remarkably effective national plans for urban development : Israel and South Africa. In both of these cases, in which Western societies exist side by side with Third World cultures, explicit goals have been formulated, pursued and achieved. For this reason they are of interest not only because of the effectiveness of the planning efforts but also because of the social theories entering into goal formulation, and the resulting changes produced in the nature of urbanisation in the two cases.

Israel: A National Plan for a 'Balanced' Urban System

The Israeli national urbanisation policy was formulated after 1948, in which year the State of Israel was created (Shachar, 1971). Before that time, a Zionist ideology prevailed that regarded the city as a necessary evil at best (Cohen, 1970). It was assumed that communal or cooperative argriculture would provide the needed national presence, and that cities were functionally unimportant.

But the choices of new immigrants belied this ideology. By 1948 three-quarters of Palestine's Jewish population lived in cities—the majority in only three cities. Fully 43.2 per cent of the national population lived in the primate city, Tel Aviv. Tel Aviv's share of industrial production, commercial enterprises, and cultural activities was even higher.

After independence large numbers of immigrants poured into the new state, including both highly skilled European city-dwellers and backward folk from both the cities and the countryside of the Middle East. Absorption of these migrants and modernisation of the traditional men were essential if growth of squatter settlements and emergence of deep socio-economic disparities between the primate city and the rest of the country were to be avoided. Thus, soon after independence, alongside absorption, five other goals of a national urbanisation policy were formulated by the new National Planning Department: settling sparsely populated regions to avoid growth of regional 'imbalances'; occupying frontier regions, for strategic purposes and to establish a national presence; opening up 'resource frontiers', particularly in the southern deserts; changing the primacy structure of the urban system by limiting the growth of urban concentration in and around Tel Aviv, and creating the 'missing' level of middle-sized towns; and building integrated regional systems of settlement by promoting complete urban hierarchies in each region.

The goal to stem the growth of Tel Aviv arose from the anti-urban Zionist ideology, and, consistent with other purposes in State building, the planners gave much stronger emphasis to social values than economic efficiency. Basic economic motives, like maximising the rate of economic growth, were not prime goals, but national sovereignty and security were.

In achieving the fourth and fifth goals, planning was based upon central-place theory, Walter Christaller's classic concept of an urban hierarchy. As one of the planners, A. Glickson, was reported to have said of the Israel for which the goals were stated by his colleague E. Brutzkus:

There were at least two Israels . . . ; the one represented by over-centralisation in three big towns and their environs, and the other represented by extreme trends of social, institutional and even economic decentralisation in small villages striving for self-sufficiency.

The planners thus decided to establish the missing middle links in the hierarchy. Settlements were divided by size into five main groups (Brutzkus, 1964) : the *basic agricultural cell* or village unit of about 500 persons; *rural centres* serving 4–6 surrounding villages with agricultural services; *urban-rural centres* with populations 6,000–12,000, serving tens of villages; *medium-sized towns* of 15,000–60,000 people, the centres of whole districts (the populated areas of the country were divided into 24 districts); *national centres* of over 100,000 people. The 'missing links' were in the middle three categories.

In the period 1948–68, 450 new rural settlements and 34 development towns were created. The new development towns accounted for 21·3 per cent of Israel's urban population by 1970.

An important underlying condition permitting such major achievement was the extent of public ownership of the land. Fully 92 per cent is controlled by the Israel Land Board (the balance being in the major existing cities and the coastal plain, controlled in its development by the powerful 1966 Planning and Building Law). No landowner has the right to develop his land other than as such right is created by an official plan. This made physical planning for the development towns much simpler in that the settler was relieved of any difficulties relating to land acquisition, property rights, and rent payments. Within this context, the basic instruments of the induced urbanisation process were two, creation of public housing and provision of employment opportunities. New housing was created by building fixed annual quotas in the development towns. New immigrants, after their initial period of citizenship training, designed to promote assimilation into the Jewish state, were directed to this housing. Rents were heavily subsidised for the first three years. The physical planners also built up the infrastructure of the new towns, and either direct public investment or financial incentives that induced private investment (including tax exemptions for several years) created job opportunities. Vocational training built up the human resources. As a result, industry in the development towns has claimed between 35 and 45 per cent of the total investment in Israel during the last decade.

By 1970 Tel Aviv's share of the national population had declined to one-third, and the primate city-size distribution had been changed to a rank-size distribution. On the other hand, the development towns have developed less intense local city–region relations than was expected, probably due to efficient transportation and the small size of the country. There have been complaints that they have higher non-European populations and greater unemployment rates than elsewhere in Israel, and that Jews of European background remain disproportionately concentrated in the major cities, and in the higher social echelons and better occupations. Because the government did not subsidise development of services in the development towns, their amenities have lagged, and heavy emigration from them into the bigger cities continues.

These caveats regarding the regional integration goal notwithstanding, it is now generally acknowledged that, in the first quarter-century of its existence, the State of Israel has been unusually successful in achieving most of the goals of the national urbanisation policy formulated in 1948 (Shachar, 1971). Reflecting on the experience, another of Israel's regional planners, E. Brutzkus, remarked at the 1971 Rehovot Conference on Urbanisation in the Developing Countries that there are real advantages from pursuing analogous policies of 'decentralised urbanisation' elsewhere in the Third World :

In social and cultural terms decentralised urbanisation makes the unavoidable transformation of traditional societies less abrupt and painful . . . than under conditions of a uniform 'modern' and cosmopolitan civilisation of a metropolitan complex. . . . The social and personal strains and sufferings linked to metropolitan concentration in the most developing countries cannot be considered as minor inconveniences versus the allegedly overriding necessities of more rapid increases in national income. It seems therefore that in most cases a policy supporting a decentralised pattern of urbanisation should be adopted.

South Africa: Control via Apartheid

While Israel sought to combat primacy and the undesirable consequences of mass immigration by creating an integrated socioeconomy and a balanced urban network, South Africa pursued a policy of separation and containment, that of *apartheid*. The context is, of course, somewhat different. Southern Africa is an outpost of European culture and settlement as well as the homeland of indigenous tribal, mainly Bantu-speaking peoples, lying athwart the boundary in contemporary world relations between the developed countries on the one hand and the Third World on the other (Fair, 1969).

The origins date back to the period of European colonial expansion, during which permanent Afrikaner and English settlements were developed, and out of which emerged 'islands' of advanced economic activity set within large but poorly endowed areas of traditional African settlement, in a classic dual economy. In 1970 the population of 21·4 million included 3·8 million White, 2·0 million Coloured, 0·6 million Asian, and 15·0 million Bantu.

To the White, sharing of political power was anathema. Many English had been schooled in the colonial tradition exemplified by Lugard's treatise *Dual Mandate* (1920). The Afrikaner had long propounded a policy of segregation, for example in the 1856 Constitution of the Transvaal (South African Republic). Thus, when the National Party came to power in 1948, many English, too, were not unhappy to see the development of an affirmative racial policy : the separate social, residential, industrial, and political development of different peoples, ensuring security for the Whites (who would not have to relinquish power to a majority of non-Whites), and leading to the separate political development of Bantu in separate vassal states. What was rejected was the growth, through migration and modernisation of the Bantu, of a multi-racial community in South Africa. Rather, the country has been divided territorially into a White state containing the major urban areas and European farming areas, and nine Bantu states, at various stages along the road to independence.

As R. J. Davies has pointed out, this policy of apartheid stems from a distinct social theory. Whereas the North American theory of the 'melting pot' in the first half of this century was that shared experiences and cooperation provide the basis for development and assimilation of migrant groups (a theory, it might be added, to which the Israelis subscribed), many South Africans have subscribed to a *friction theory*. This theory holds that physical, social, cultural, and economic differences between peoples are fundamentally incompatible, leading to friction on contact, and thus that harmonious relations between groups can be secured only by reducing the points of contact to a minimum, particularly in the cities, creating a mosaic of social worlds which coexist without penetration—a situation which we noted has been the actual American experience in recent years.

Eighty-seven per cent of the Whites live in towns, including large numbers of previously poor Afrikaners, next after the English to urbanise before Asians, Coloureds and Blacks, and the greatest supporters of the National Party. But these same urban areas which in 1936 contained 1·36 million Whites, 0·4 million Coloureds, 0·52 million Asians and 1·24 million Bantu by 1970 contained 3·3 million Whites, 1·5 million Coloureds, 0·54 million Asians, and 4·99 million Bantu. Non-Whites now comprise two-thirds of the urban population. As this change took place, it signalled the threat to which the White Afrikaner responded by accelerating government action to halt the growth of an integrated multi-racial society. Non-Whites were denied political representation in White areas. By colour bar legislation, better-paying skilled jobs were reserved for Whites (see Fig. 12). The Bantu was denied

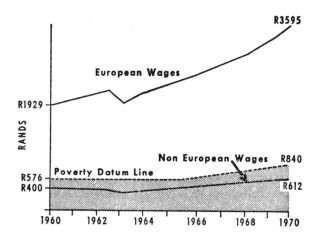

FIG. 12   Incomes of black and white South Africans relative to the poverty line

permanent status in White areas. Influx control restricted Bantu migrations to the employment needs of industry and services. The residential areas of cities were segregated.

Influx control was undertaken in earnest after the Second World War. The post-war period brought Bantu workers flooding into peripheral squatter settlements, or crowding into factory barracks. Successive measures tightened controls upon immigrants until by 1957 the principle was laid down that only Bantus born in urban areas who had lived there continuously, or who had been in unbroken employment for ten years, or had been lawfully resident there for fifteen years without leaving the area, were entitled to remain. These measures were designed to prevent the establishment of a large permanent urban Bantu society, and also to perpetuate the supply to the towns of temporary workers in demand by growing industries, eager for pools of cheap labour.

By 1964 the measures were strengthened further. *All* Bantu in the White areas were now to be regarded as temporary residents whose permanent homes lay in the Bantu 'Homelands', to which they could be compelled to return if unemployed or if their presence was deemed undesirable. As a result, Bantu migration to the cities has been controlled in a way not paralleled elsewhere.

Within the urban areas, the different racial groups have been segregated, producing radical transformations in the racial ecology of the cities. In 1958, it was estimated that the full achievement of apartheid would require movement of 50 per cent of the Coloured, 50 per cent of the Indian, 67 per cent of the Bantu and 20 per cent of the White population. By 1970 the sought-after segregation involving such shifts had largely been achieved. The apartheid city contains consolidated group areas that avoid ethnic 'islands', and provide 'protection' in the form of either physical or man-made barriers separating the groups. Direct access to work zones is provided along routes that wherever possible do not involve passage through any other group's territory. Non-White areas are, generally, located close to major industrial foci, with sectoral orientation towards the native homelands where these impinge upon metropolitan areas, as at Pretoria and Durban.

In the cities the Bantu is denied land ownership. Through slum clearance and rehousing schemes, Bantu squatter settlements have been removed and new Bantu residential areas have been created on the peripheries of the White cities. The only exception is that one Bantu servant is allowed to reside on the property of each White household, and the servants in apartment buildings in the city centres live hidden on the rooftops in 'reservations in the sky'. In the Witwatersrand Metropolitan Area surrounding Johannesburg, Soweto (the South-western Native Townships) housed over 500,000 Bantu in 1970, in row upon row of identical homes physically superior to the former Bantu squatter slums, arranged in groupings that preserve tribal organisation (Holzner, 1971). In Durban, Indians were removed from more desirable residential settings to be replaced by Europeans. Of an Asian population of 250,000, over 60 per cent will have been relocated by 1975. And in Cape Town more than 100,000 of the Coloured population were removed from the central city and resettled in the less desirable Cape Flats. Current plans call for the development of a separate Coloured city at Mamre, 50 kilometres north of Cape Town, designed to have a population of 800,000 by the turn of the century.

A keystone in the policy of apartheid is the creation of the nine 'Bantustans' as vassal Black states. These are supposedly independently governed permanent homelands from which the urban workers are presumed to have migrated as work-seekers, not settlers, but are, in fact, strictly controlled native reservations. To the Afrikaner regional planner, an urban decentralisation or 'growth centres' policy means one in which considerable incentives are offered to industry to locate in boundary areas between the homelands and the White areas. In this way, Bantu labour can live in the homeland and work in the White factories, thus solving one of the continuing dilemmas of the metropolises—maintaining an apartheid policy while satisfying growing needs for industrial employment. Thus, a major industrial complex has been created at Rossyln between Pretoria and an adjacent reservation, and similar arrangements have been created in Durban. Where boundary locations are not possible, as in the gold mines of the Orange Free State or the diamond mines of South West Africa (Namibia), black male workers are housed in dormitory compounds segregated by tribe and clan, to enable older males to maintain traditional social controls over the young men.

To date, these policies designed to cast the joint processes of urbanisation and modernisation that are occurring elsewhere in the world into purposively segregated forms have been quite effective. Normal migration mechanisms have been interdicted and the fuller participation of the majority Black group in South African society has been checked, a system of temporary labour migration has been prolonged, and vast numbers have been moved to segregate the cities. While systems of incentives have induced shifts in industrial location to 'growth centres', and while within European areas development has proceeded in directions commensurate with the western model, checked only by the public counterpoint of town planning British-style, the overriding achievement has been accomplished by the coercive application of police power and by thought control—of the curriculum in the schools, textbooks, broadcast news, and the like. As the *Rand Daily Mail* said despairingly on 24 June 1972, in a public debate over a textbook 're-interpreting' South African history being imposed on the schools :

Why is such a book approved for the children? The answer lies in the Nationalist drive to retain rule over this country by moulding the thinking of the people of South Africa to a predetermined cast. The Whites must fear all who are of a different colour or philosophy or political outlook. And in accordance with the underlying principle of Christian National Education, even the Whites themselves, while remaining together in the laager, must still stay in their separate English and Afrikaans camps. For Africans, Coloureds and Indians this is equally well-defined : they must know their limited place in life. This is the bitter reality of our situation.

4 Planning for New Urban Realities: The Post-War European Experiences

INDUSTRIAL urbanisation came earlier to Britain and adjacent north-western Europe than it did to North America. As early as 1843, Robert Vaughan could proclaim in Britain that 'ours is the age of great cities'. From 1801 to 1911, Britain's urban areas accounted for 94 per cent of the country's population increase. One-third of the urban growth was due to net immigration from rural areas (Lawton, 1972). Industrialisation lagged in its onset eastward into the Slavic cultures and southward into the Mediterranean lands, however. There, older urban forms have persisted to the present. Indeed, throughout Europe the impact of industrial urbanisation was felt through screens of social structure and an urban inheritance from earlier times. As a result, many of its human consequences have differed from those in North America. In turn, these consequences produced a major turning point in the western urbanisation experience after the Second World War, as public policies began to shape sought-after urban futures. It was in Europe that the strategies of deliberate urbanisation to which the countries of the Third World aspire were developed and have had the greatest effect.

THE URBAN INHERITANCE

It is well that we begin by reviewing the differing European context within which modern urbanisation took place, before we turn to the attempts to plan new urban forms and social structures in the last quarter of a century, because it was these prior urban inheritances that produced the differing goals sought after by the planners.

Lichtenberger (1970) argues that it is possible to distinguish at least four historic city types in Europe, each a product of different determinants of form and structure : the medieval burgher city of the feudal territorial state; the city of the nobility, a creation of the absolutist state; the industrial city of the liberal laissez-faire period; and the New Town of the social welfare state and socialist system. Even in the latter case she points out significant differences between Eastern and Western Europe. Whether or not this is a proper classification, it does suggest a variety of forms absent from the American scene and makes it critical to review the differing range of inherited urban patterns and social ecologies in Europe, the differing tradition of public involvement in the cities, including a longer-standing concern with civic design, and differing domestic architecture and housing preferences. Each of these will be discussed in turn.

Urban Patterns and Social Structure

The physical skeleton of the European city was seldom the expression of economic forces played out on a rectangular grid, as it had been in most of North America. (Principal activity centres and landmarks even today reflect earlier religious values, as in the case of cathedrals, churches and monasteries, or political organisation, as in the town halls of autonomous medieval cities, palaces of the ruler in the baroque period, or the culture palaces of the present socialist states.) Seldom, until well into the twentieth century, did economic institutions such as corporation headquarters, banks or financial institutions, assume any centrality in European urban structure.

By North American standards, the street pattern of most European cities appears as a complicated patchwork too, comprehensible only upon laborious town plan analysis. In most cases, the radial long-distance roads from the old gateways of the medieval town provided the basic skeleton filled in by later developments that respected earlier rural settlement patterns and field boundaries. Planted avenues, which became popular in the baroque period, did not always make for a better organisation of the ground plan. They were partly fitted into the older street pattern, partly oriented to monumental buildings and they sometimes ended as cul-de-sacs in the countryside. They did, however, add new radial elements to the urban landscape in many European cities. Boulevards which replaced the medieval fortifications in the nineteenth century are frequently the only circular thoroughfares.

Plazas belong to the significant inventory of European open space. Wherever they date back to medieval market places, they are still nodes of urban activity. And the traditional city centres have preserved their attraction through many processes of change, always adapting to new economic circumstances.

Wall and moat were also expressions of urban existence from the classical period to the modern era. The gateways functioned as control posts both for the traffic of people and goods, and served as tax stations as well. Fortifications possessed other than military importance too, forming an essential social and economic barrier between city and suburbs. Higher social prestige as well as different economic activities separated the burghers of the city from the inhabitants of the suburbs, and a gradient of social status and wealth from the centre to the periphery was common, being preserved in the twentieth century more frequently in continental Europe than in Britain.

Throughout most of the history of European cities, their skyline was strictly controlled by plans going back to the fire regulations of the Middle Ages. In Paris the building height was fixed at 20 metres in 1795. During the nineteenth century this example was imitated by the other big European cities. London preserved the dominance in its skyline of St Paul's Cathedral. Therefore, steel and cement technology did not change the look of the central areas of cities, as it did in North America. Until recently skyscraper construction has been subject to special controls, although the recent changes in regulations in Paris and London are now widely decried for their devastating effect on former vistas. The consequence of these restrictions should not be underestimated. The land value peak of the Central Business District was suppressed and could not be reflected in office towers and other highrise buildings as in North America. The development of the core area had to take place in a different way. Instead, the old city within the wall—the city as it had existed before urban expansion in the industrial age—became the urban core in which were concentrated the administrative, financial, commercial, cultural and amusement facilities of the city. This inner city is sometimes still defined by its former walls, as at York and Canterbury in England or Nürnberg in Germany, or more frequently by the ring of boulevards that has replaced the walls, around which the modern skyscraper development has more recently been permitted.

The classical pre-industrial European city also had a distinctive socio-spatial structure. First, the process of urban growth brought about the incorporation of suburbs, villages, and small towns into the urban area. Melding into the densely built-up area, they maintained their distinct socio-economic features, retaining their own landmarks and shopping streets. The local spirit was reflected in the identification of the inhabitants with their specific quarters. During the second half of the nineteenth century modern administrations often combined several such units into one district, taking into account the socio-economic peculiarities. City-like communities outside of the city boundaries were annexed and transformed into districts. Such districts possessed or gained not only a specific social image but also their own institutions and retail centres.

Overarching this structure of quarters and districts was the city-wide pattern alluded to earlier which could, according to J. G. Kohl (1841) be viewed as a series of 'layers', as in Fig. 13 : (1) the

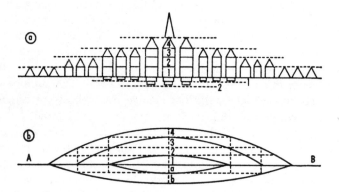

F IG. 13   Socio-economic structure of European cities in the mid-nineteenth century, according to J. G. Kohl

ground floor (*Rez-de-Chausée*) containing the establishments and living quarters of the businessmen; (2) the first floor (*Bel Étage*), the 'area of wealth and pleasure', the seat of the nobility; (3)–(5) 'upwards', people with lower income reside; and the same applying to the subterranean levels, (a) and (b). These layers, Kohl said, translated into 'arches' of social structure, so that the economic and social importance of the population also declined with distance from the centre of the city.

That the implied heterogeneity of the inner city was possible in the European city on a floor-by-floor basis within buildings was undoubtedly due to class systems with well-marked status distinctions in dress, speech and manner, and well-defined systems of etiquette and deference that defined and preserved social distances. Only to the extent that class systems become more fluid and social distinctions less clear does it become necessary to preserve status differences by spatial segregation, as in the highly mobile American city (Berghe, 1960). Thus, social and spatial distances are substitutes for one another, the first defining and maintaining status differences in a stable class system in which status is inherited and in which residential areas may be heterogeneous, and the second protecting achieved status in a society with a greater degree of social mobility, providing safety from possible status threats only in the social homogeneity of neighbourhoods and communities.

Industrialisation came to places with inherited socio-spatial structures of the kind described by Kohl rather than creating cities *de novo*, or was grafted on to small rural market towns. There was no planning of industrial urbanisation in the birth place of the industrial metropolis, Great Britain, nor very much of it in the later developments on the continent. The densities of the walled-in medieval towns were maintained in the newer expansion because of the limitations of horse and foot on movement (Wells, 1902), the need for face-to-face contacts to conduct business, and the fact that such building regulations as were applied to the new developments were those of the old city. But because the new industrial order brought greater social mobility, it also produced greater spatial segregation.

To Britain, the Victorian metropolis brought new factories and workshops, and, to handle the products of the new specialisation, port facilities and railway terminals adjacent to the old city, which became the commercial core and the symbol of the new urbanisation. In association with the railway termini and docks were to be found the wholesale warehouses and retail commodity markets, and separating the old city from the newer residential developments were the factories and workshops. Horse-drawn city transport, and later the suburban railways and tramways, gave rise to better-quality suburban development in areas previously beyond walking distance from the centre. The character of the suburbs owed much to the pattern of communications, the pre-existing types of residential areas within the city, and the nature of land ownership in the areas under development. In Britain, the first to move out of the city were the middle classes, to single family homes in new suburbs, thus breaking the older tradition of the pre-industrial city in which the workers' suburbs were peripheral, often beyond the walls. This move was not paralleled extensively elsewhere in Europe, however, where to this day 'suburb' frequently implies lower class and where the historic claims of centrality and the preference for apartment living still conspire to contain many continental cities to more restricted areas.

It is this difference, emerging as it did in the mid-nineteenth century, that Choay (1965) has argued is the source of the two dominant ideologies in European urban planning in this century. British new towns concepts sought a new balance of town and country reflecting the new middle-class orientation to the suburbs and beyond, whereas the French *grand ensemble* focused on the apartment house and on the higher density living it represents. To Choay, the work of Ebenezer Howard, Lewis Mumford and Frank Lloyd Wright on the one hand, and Le Corbusier on the other, exemplify these two main currents of thought; in this sense Wright's *Broadacre City* is the ultimate in decentralisation of the family house, whereas Le Corbusier's *Ville Radieuse* is the archetype of vertical steel and glass apartment towers, cruciform in shape, elevated on stilts and with wide pedestrian spaces between.

In both Victorian Britain and Continental Europe, housing for the new factory workers was built in courts, back from the street, confined, poorly-lit, ill-ventilated and lacking even rudimentary water supplies and sanitation. Often, cellars were used as dwellings to increase the housing capacity.

A graphic picture of the urban ecology and social structure of the times in Britain was provided by Friedrich Engels in 1844 :

Manchester contains, at its heart, a rather extended commercial district, perhaps half a mile long and about as broad, and consisting almost wholly of offices and warehouses. Nearly the whole district is abandoned by dwellers, and is lonely and deserted at night. . . . The district is cut through by certain main thoroughfares upon which the vast traffic concentrates, and in which the ground level is lined with brilliant shops. In these streets the upper floors are occupied, here and there, and there is a good deal of life upon them until late at night. With the exception of this commercial district, all Manchester proper, all Salford and Hulme . . . are all unmixed working people's quarters, stretching like a girdle, averaging a mile and a half in breadth, around the commercial district. Outside, beyond this girdle, lives the upper and middle bourgeoisie in regularly laid out streets in the vicinity of working quarters . . . the upper bourgeoisie in remoter villas with gardens . . . in free, wholesome country air, in fine, comfortable homes, passed every half or quarter hour by omnibuses going into the city. And the finest part of the arrangement is this, that the members of the money aristocracy can take the shortest road through the middle of all the labouring districts without ever seeing that they are in the midst of the grimy misery that lurks to the right and left. For the thoroughfares leading from the Exchange in all directions out of the city are lined, on both sides, with an almost unbroken series of shops, and are so kept in the hands of the middle and lower bourgeoisie . . . [that] they suffice to conceal from the eyes of the wealthy men and women of strong stomachs and weak nerves the misery and grime which form the complement of their wealth. . . . I know very well that this hypocritical plan is more or less common to all great cities; I know, too, that the retail dealers are forced by the nature of their business to take possession of the great highways; I know that there are more good buildings than bad ones upon such streets everywhere, and that the value of land is greater near them than in remote districts; but at the same time, I have never seen so systematic a shutting out of the working class from the thoroughfares, so tender a concealment of everything which might affront the eye and the nerves of the bourgeoisie, as in Manchester. And yet, in other respects, Manchester is less built according to plan after official regulations, is more outgrowth of accident, than any other city; and when I consider in this connection the eager assurances of the middle class, that the working class is doing famously, I cannot help feeling that the liberal manufacturers, the Big Wigs of Manchester, are not so innocent after all, in the matter of this sensitive method of construction.

The spatial organisation described by Engels is quite analogous to the one described later for the North American industrial metropolis by R. E. Park and E. W. Burgess (1925), and because of its ills, it not only became anathema to the socialist ideologues of the later nineteenth century, but was the source of the same succession of reform movements already noted in the American case. Epidemic disease was prevalent, and produced in Britain the Sanitary Reform Movement. Significant events in this movement included Edwin Chadwick's report on the *Sanitary Condition of the Labouring Population* in 1842, the Royal Commission on the Health of the Towns in 1843, the Public Health Act of 1848, and compulsory powers to enforce reforms under the Public Health Acts of 1872 and 1875.

Linked with the drive for better public health was the felt need for public decision-making to control the deleterious consequences of private interests thought to be selfishly exploiting the tenement-bound working poor. Housing codes were thus linked to environmental controls for public health purposes and to the creation of good quality low-cost housing. As a result, environmental standards were gradually improved. Housing standards were formulated and enforced, sanitary sewers were constructed, streets were paved, refuse disposal was brought under control. After the Housing Act of 1890, local councils in Britain were permitted to replace slums by good housing. In Britain, Germany and Belgium, effective means of creating a low-cost housing supply were being developed—charitable trusts, for example, pioneered by investing in limited-profit, reasonable-rental flats—and slum clearance and housing programmes under municipal direction were developed.

The slum clearance programmes were not without their opponents and radical critiques even in the nineteenth century, however. Demolition and redevelopment for commercial, railroad and monumental public purposes pushed older working-class residences out of slums in and around the town centres. In Britain, there was concern for the abysmal living conditions and housing of the poor, but again Engels remarked :

In reality the bourgeoisie has only one method of solving the housing question after *its* fashion—that is to say, of solving it in such a way that the solution continually reproduces itself anew. This method is called 'Haussmann'. . . . By 'Haussmann' I mean the practice which has now become general of making breaches in the working class quarters of our big towns, and particularly in areas which are centrally situated, quite apart from whether this is done from considerations of public health and for beautifying the town, or owing to the demand for big centrally situated business premises, or owing to traffic requirements, such as the laying down of railways, streets (which sometimes appear to have the strategic aim of making barricade fighting more difficult). . . . No matter how different the reasons may be, the result is everywhere the same; the scandalous alleys disappear to the accompaniment of lavish self-praise from the bourgeoisie on account of the tremendous success, but they appear again immediately somewhere else and often in the immediate neighbourhood ! . . . The breeding places of disease, the infamous holes and cellars in which the capitalist mode of production confines our workers night after night, are not abolished; they are merely *shifted elsewhere* ! The same economic necessity which produced them in the first place, produces them in the next place also. As long as the capitalist mode of production continues to exist, it is folly to hope for an isolated solution to the housing question or of any other social question affecting the fate of the workers. The solution lies in the abolition of the capitalist mode of production and the appropriation of all the means of life and labour by the working class itself.

Out of the condition of the working classes arose the various reform movements that were to have their expression in the built form and social structure of the twentieth-century European metropolis.

One of these was the New Towns Movement. In Ebenezer Howard's mind, the new town was to achieve three goals : (1) rearrangement of the inhuman mass of the big industrial city on a human scale in new towns of strictly limited size; (2) balance between the quantity of housing and the number of jobs; and (3) public ownership of the land to paralyse speculation and thereby control development. In this way, public intervention was to be used to counter the human consequences of laissez-faire industrial urbanisation.

The Tradition of Public Involvement
The public role has, of course, been present throughout European urban history. The medieval city-community performed a wide range of functions, as the greater number of public buildings demonstrates. The architecture of the town hall, normally occupying the central plaza, was an outward sign of the importance of a city. The City Council controlled the economic activity of the burghers, and also collected taxes. It had the responsibility of providing food supply in case of emergency, as is evidenced by public storage buildings such as the salt towers, flour houses and bread houses. Religious orders participated in social services and schooling.

The absolutist state superimposed its administration on that of the city, particularly in the national capitals, where municipal authority sank to the role of handmaiden to the state government. Above all cultural institutions—universities, museums, theatres—became an obligation of the ruler.

Liberalism created autonomous community legislation. Step by step city councils increased their range of functions. Old, half-forgotten ideas of responsibility for housing, schooling, welfare, etc. gave rise to municipal socialism. The idea of municipal self-administration brought early control over utilities such as gas, electricity, and the public transportation system. The municipality often became the biggest entrepreneur in town.

The non-profit policy for delivering many services formed one cornerstone of this municipal socialism, and welfare programmes a second. Extensive urban planning, a third ingredient, demanded power to dispose of the land freely to be effective. The Prussian kings realised this when trying to remodel Berlin in the eighteenth century. Purchasing one lot after another they succeeded in acquiring 40 per cent of the city area. New social democratic city governments imitated this example. As early as 1910 Stockholm started to acquire lots and forest areas inside and outside of the former city boundaries, and this provided the basis for radical new ventures in city building after the Second World War.

Concern with Civic Design

Design, also, has always played a leading role in the European city. Drawings of the sixteenth and seventeenth centuries show how architectural design reflected spiritual values, religious ideas and political order. The strict rules of social organisation of the burgher community are manifest in the way their individually built residences formed a continuous united façade. Even the fortifications combined military expediency with representation.

The baroque court city, in particular, strengthened this principle in a monumental manner. Imposing avenues leading to palaces and public buildings became an instrument of architectural design. The integration of parks into the urban landscape laid the foundation for an important tradition. As large avenues of trees demonstrate, the dimensions of the baroque city were no longer adjusted to pedestrians, but to riders and carriages. The house of the citizen played a subordinate role in this concept. Everywhere in West and Central Europe, palatial architecture was imitated by the middle class. The bourgeoisie built in the way the nobility did.

This development led to the 'façade culture' in Continental West and Central Europe. In this era not only the tenement houses of the middle class, but even those of blue collar people, were ornamented with elements taken from a wide range of historical styles. At the same time, the idea of state representation crested in the capitals of the large countries. The remodelling of Paris by Haussmann was imitated in particular by Belgian and Spanish urban architecture.

This period of the late nineteenth century, modifying the older physical pattern as no earlier era had done, activated other forces too. In the decades of the worst land speculation, preservation campaigns started. As early as 1907 a law against the disfigurement of settlements had been passed in Prussia. Ever since, the preservation idea has been an important factor in European city planning programmes.

Under municipal socialism, large-scale housing programmes first appeared in Vienna in the early 1920s. The castle-like character of the building masses reflected the strong opposition faced by this new concept, but helped it to gain worldwide interest. Imitated by other cities, the impressive design was lost and only the huge building size was retained as, for example, in Glasgow. It remained for Stockholm to lead progress in social housing programmes, adding architectural attractiveness to economic efficiency.

Landscape architecture was an integral element of the absolutist urban concept. Originally reserved for the privileged upper class, mainly the nobility, many parks were opened to the public during the Age of Enlightenment. In many cities the demolition of fortifications created a green belt around the old town. Its design and upkeep became the duty of the municipal board. During the period of Liberalism, the common land concept of the medieval community coalesced with the aesthetic principle of the baroque garden-culture. The master plans of the late nineteenth century already fitted some public parks into the closely built-up areas. Private gardens were purchased and made accessible for the public. Municipal housing programmes initiated the idea of the 'social green' with a playground for children and other recreational facilities. The model created was imitated by co-operative and freehold housing development all over Europe after the Second World War.

In this context, the Continental green belt concept, formulated first in Vienna in 1904, can be understood. It was thought of as a recreation area for people living in the densely built-up city. The green belt also became an instrument for controlling urban growth, and for subdividing the urban pattern into neighbourhoods, as in

Ottawa, Canada. Green belts can be found in the master plans of many European cities. Their preservation depends on the opportunities for controlling land speculation, which are not the same throughout Europe.

Domestic Architecture and Housing Preferences

The history of domestic architecture in Continental Europe is dominated by the apartment house rather than by the single-family residence arranged in terraces, semi-detached, or detached as in Britain. On the Continent, the apartment house had appeared during the Renaissance. New residential properties for the well-to-do were designed as multi-storey apartment houses with arcaded patios. Standardised large-scale tenement blocks did not become profitable investments for bankers, entrepreneurs and wholesalers until the mid-eighteenth century, however. Naples stands as a prototype. To this day these huge tenement houses characterise Naples' urban core. The same social class of wealthy bourgeoisie residing in spacious apartments on the second floors of their tenement houses in the large continental cities showed a completely different residential pattern in England, though. In London's West End (Bloomsbury, Mayfair, Belgravia, Regent's Park), large-scale developers had leased tracts of land from the Crown and some of the old aristocratic families and built attractive terraces of single-family mansions, available on long-term leases, around private open-space in central squares. Thus, two different residential images of the upper middle class were initiated which significantly differentiated subsequent British and European development styles, as we noted earlier.

During the second half of the eighteenth century the tenement house spread to medium-sized Continental cities, where it was frequently an offshoot of the craftsman's townhouse. The long wings, originally used for workshops or storage, were converted into tiny flats. These older tenement houses at first supplied the demands of the middle-income group. The barracks for tenants in the lowest social strata were the offsprings of the industrial revolution, created by the laissez-faire housing market. Construction companies carried out the parcelling of the lots. Agents and real estate offices handled the transactions; mortgage banks took over credit arrangements. Tenement house property became an attractive capital investment for wealthy people. Capitals such as Paris,

Berlin and Vienna created distinct prototypes that were imitated by smaller provincial cities.

Just as industrialisation appeared only in outposts in east central European agricultural landscapes, the tenement house was not found there at all outside the capitals and some industrial cities. Instead, most cities and towns kept their semi-rural appearance, with traditional one storey row-houses providing most of the housing.

The First World War brought vast changes in the urban system throughout Europe. The freezing of rents by Tenement Protection Laws, the 'social rents' of the welfare housing programmes, non-profit construction by co-operatives, and the economic rent of the freehold apartment changed the dwelling market and created an increasingly complicated structure. During the interwar period the apartment house was adopted by social welfare programmes without becoming an instrument for segregating the poor, as it did later in North American slum clearance projects. Indeed, the majority of apartment houses on the European continent continued to be built for all income strata. Before the elevator came into widespread use, the best apartments always occupied the second and third floors. There were also contrasts between the large front apartments and the small flats looking out to the backyards. A further restriction on segregation resulted from the fact that the housing was often controlled, not by profit-seeking landlords or large construction companies, but by governmental housing agencies.

Thus, by and large, European dwelling structure developed along lines different from those in North America. The self-employed practiced only partial separation of living and working, particularly trades people and small-scale entrepreneurs if they owned the property housing their enterprise. Mass production of tenement houses did, of course, create the problem of tiny flats poorly equipped but durably constructed. Social housing programmes, oriented towards the demands of the poor, tried to build at low cost as many dwellings as possible to cope with perennial housing shortages. Even in the last two decades, the average dwelling size has increased very slowly. Housing development still lags behind the rising demand for better equipped dwellings of larger size. In this fact resides much of the power of planning. So long as housing shortages remain, the freedom of choice of consumers is restricted. If the available housing is allocated according to a plan, it becomes the means of ensuring that the goals of the plan are achieved.

BRITAIN'S NEW TOWNS: THE SEARCH FOR AN ALTERNATIVE TO INDUSTRIAL URBANISATION

Disaffection with industrial urbanisation came earliest in Britain, and finally found other than experimental physical expression in the landscape after the Second World War, when the role of the state in management of national economy and society moved to the forefront throughout Europe (Harrison, 1968). By 1971 the population of 22 British new and expanded towns, begun since 1947, was already more than 1·2 million, occupying more than 250,000 new homes. The towns employed almost 600,000 workers. By the end of the century, the 28 currently designated new and expanded towns are expected to account for some 4 per cent of the national population of 65 to 75 millions, although this figure may increase as the result of Britain's new strategic plans for regional development.

The New Towns Policy can be attributed to many things, but among the most potent are two sources of opposition to laissez-faire in the use of land: the strong aristocratic tradition of *noblesse oblige*, and the strength of welfare socialism. There has been much less sympathy in Britain than in North America for speculative land use and urban development, for the British aristocratic tradition stresses responsibilities far more than rights. And from the onset of industrial urbanisation there has been continuing concern for the employment of the working class and the living conditions of the poor, although again, and judging by such figures as the number of homeless in the Victorian city, concern frequently fell far short of need. Thus, the development of the post-war plans for Britain's new towns must be seen in light of the country's earlier history of social and physical planning that emerged in large measure *as a human consequence* of nineteenth-century urbanisation.

Early Growth of British Planning
Both the aristocratic and the welfare concerns can be seen in the growth of British planning practice from the eighteenth century

on (Cherry, 1972). Good design was implicit in the paternalistic influences that gave order to urban settlements in the eighteenth century, and resulted in Georgian squares in London and the Royal Crescent in Bath. Early industrial urbanisation did, of course, breed the squalor of the laissez-faire Victorian city, decried by Engels when he wrote of 'dwellings of the workers everywhere badly planned, badly built, and kept in the worst condition, badly ventilated, damp and unwholesome'. But such conditions brought the drive for sanitary regulation that culminated by 1875 in a nation-wide public health service network. At the same time, philanthropic housing associations began to seek good housing for the poor, while social reformers and visionaries and radical reform movements all gained strength. From Henry Mayhew to Charles Booth to Seebohm Rowntree, a new type of social analyst and commentator highlighted the conditions of the poor, while the activism of the social Christians in the Salvation Army, and of agitation for more equity in the distribution of wealth gained strength. Paralleling America's Progressive movement, there was a strong drive in Britain for the creation of a more humane and national civic community. Some social reformers became practical experimenters in the tradition of Robert Owen, and the idea of new model towns as alternatives to uncontrolled urbanisation gained strength. Enlightened factory owners such as the Cadbury Brothers built Bournville, and Port Sunlight was built by Lever as a rival model township. The climate at the end of the nineteenth century was marked by a continuing disquiet at the size of London that dated at least from Elizabethan times, deep concern about poverty and poor housing, and a strong sense of escaping to alternatives.

It was in this climate that Ebenezer Howard helped to shape British urban history. In 1898 he published his book *Tomorrow: A Peaceful Path to Real Reform*, revised in 1902 as *Garden Cities of Tomorrow*. Later, Howard said :

The essential aim of the Garden City in my mind was this : it was to unite people of good will, irrespective of creed or party, in worthy purpose—the building of a city on juster, saner, healthier, and more efficient lines than the cities of the old order.

His main concern was the plight of the over-crowded cities and depleted country districts, and he concluded that there were not just two alternatives—town life and country life—but a third alternative—town life in a country setting 'in perfect combination'. Working with the distinguished planner Raymond Unwin, he developed and built the first garden city at Letchworth in 1903 as a 'city in a garden'. Later, with F. J. Osborn and C. B. Purdom involved, the Garden Cities and Town Planning Association led in the construction of Welwyn Garden City in 1920.

But the First World War intervened, and after the war Britain was faced with an immense housing shortage, and it was agreed that the private sector was incapable of meeting housing needs at rents people could pay. Housing Acts in 1919 and 1924 enabled Local Authorities to build and plan public housing estates. From 1919 to the mid-thirties, local authority housing and other state-aided construction accounted for about one-half of all new housing, as they do today, and a major policy aim had emerged : to provide satisfactory housing for all at rents within their capacity to pay. Most of the new public housing programmes lacked broader planning content, however, and the private sector of the housing industry, relatively unconstrained, produced increasing urban sprawl radiating from towns in the form of speculative profit-seeking ribbon developments responding to the demands of Britons for homes in the countryside. In response to such speculation came a succession of Town Planning Acts, the most important being that of 1932, which authorised local governments 'to control development; to secure proper statutory conditions—amenity and convenience; to preserve existing buildings. . . .' Local Authorities were authorised to zone land and to reserve land from development; both of these ingredients were to assume major post-war importance in controlling urban form.

The social impact of these changes was substantial. Indeed, Robson (1969) has concluded that 'in the twentieth century, the development of council housing and of town planning . . . have largely invalidated many of the bases on which the classical models (i.e. Wirth) have been built'. He refers to the lower spatial and social mobility in British cities, the critical importance of the local area as a facet of the individual's social world, involving significant face-to-face relationships and kinship networks, the persuasive influence of age structure on social outlook in housing estates where early occupants stayed and aged together, and the continuing importance of more rigid social class roles in the British way of life. Each of these factors was to play its role in post-war

Britain, just as they had converged to create new life styles in the council house estates.

But in 1932 Britain was still experiencing the mass unemployment brought on by the Great Depression, although that year saw the beginning of the upturn in trade and finance. At the time that A. Trystan Edwards was circulating proposals for a hundred new towns widely spread throughout the country, and at the time in 1935 that the London County Council appropriated £2 million for acquisition of land as part of a green belt system, the Royal Commission on the Distribution of the Industrial Population was created under the chairmanship of Sir Montague Barlow. The Barlow Report was delayed by the beginning of the Second World War. When published in 1940, it recommended controlling London's growth, redevelopment of congested urban areas, decentralisation or dispersal of industry and population from such areas, the encouragement of 'balanced' regional growth, and to achieve the last two, creation of garden cities or garden suburbs, satellite towns, trading estates, and the development of existing small towns and outlying regional centres. Sir Patrick Abercrombie was one of six members of the Barlow Commission signing minority reports urging stronger recommendations and a New Towns Policy, which he subsequently helped fashion.

The Post-war Plans: New Towns
The war resulted in widespread devastation, especially in London. But as early as October 1940, Lord Reith had been appointed Minister of Works and Buildings, and in March 1941 he asked the London County Council to prepare plans for post-war reconstruction. The LCC hired Patrick Abercrombie to work as consultant with the Council's architect, J. H. Forshaw. The result was *The County of London Plan* (1943). Abercrombie pictured London in concentric-ring terms. The inner ring was to have population and industry reduced. A surrounding suburban ring required no action. This was girdled by a green belt in which urban growth was to be stopped. Finally, in the surrounding country ring, the planned expansion of existing towns and eight totally new towns were to house overspill population and industry, 525,000 in the planned expansions and 350,000 in the new towns. Many of his population assumptions have been shown to be

wildly astray but, nevertheless, Abercrombie's ideal guided post-war planning, supported by the 1943 and 1944 Town and Country Planning Acts that strengthened the machinery for intervention and control of private development by the system of planning permissions. A new Labour Government came to power after the war with a landslide majority, and enthusiastic commitment to planning, ideological opposition to profit-seeking development, and left-over wartime controls, most notably the complete control of all building licences.

Planning could proceed affirmatively because most housing was to be publicly built, new construction was to be licensed in accordance with national investment priorities, while physical design was to be an instrument of the new social policy. Plans were made at all levels of government and powers were provided for their implementation.

In 1945 Lord Reith was appointed to chair an Advisory Committee to the Minister of Town and Country Planning

to consider the general questions of the establishment, development organisation and administration that will arise in the promotion of New Towns in furtherance of a policy of planned decentralisation from congested urban areas; and . . . to suggest guiding principles on which such towns should be established and developed as self-contained and balanced communities for work and living.

Three reports were prepared, and culminated in the New Towns Act of 1946.

Between 1946 and 1949 eight new towns were designated for Greater London, including Stevenage, Crawley and Hemel Hempstead. The 'web' of approaches comprising doctrine in this planning effort for London has been described by Donald L. Foley (1963). Foley's diagram is reproduced here as Fig. 14. At the national level the main social goal was maintenance of full employment, from which were obtained derivative programme goals such as the redistribution of employment to areas of high unemployment, made possible by the supporting approach of industrial development certificates. At the regional planning level the main goal related to the physical organisation of the London region, while at the town planning level the goal was to create the best possible living conditions for the population. A strong 'containment' intent permeated the effort; crowded inner areas were to

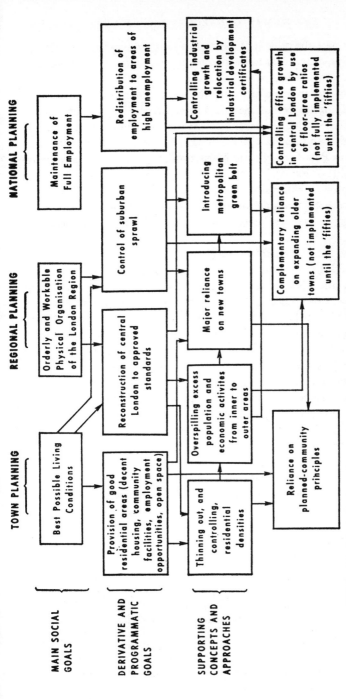

NOTE: Asterisks indicate goals, programmes and approaches particularly permeated with 'containment' intent.

FIG. 14 The web of approaches comprising the Doctrine for Planning London

The original version of this diagram was prepared by Donald L. Foley in his evaluation of the British planning experience.

TOWN PLANNING

REGIONAL PLANNING

NATIONAL PLANNING

MAIN SOCIAL GOALS

Best Possible Living Conditions

Orderly and Workable Physical Organisation of the London Region

Maintenance of Full Employment

DERIVATIVE AND PROGRAMMATIC GOALS

Provision of good residential areas (decent housing, community facilities, employment opportunities, open space)

Reconstruction of central London to approved standards

Control of suburban sprawl

Redistribution of employment to areas of high unemployment

SUPPORTING CONCEPTS AND APPROACHES

Thinning out, and controlling, residential densities

Overspilling excess population and economic activities from inner to outer areas

Major reliance on new towns

Introducing metropolitan green belt

Controlling industrial growth and relocation by industrial development certificates

Reliance on planned-community principles

Complementary reliance on expanding older towns (not implemented until the 'fifties)

Controlling office growth in central London by use of floor-area ratios (not fully implemented until the 'fifties)

be thinned, the growth of the core of London was to be contained, and new growth was to be directed into socially and economically balanced new towns of limited scale.

Since the initial plans were drawn, the number of new towns actively under development has been increased to 22, including a later stage of higher density towns such as Cumbernauld outside Glasgow, and a new phase of massive extensions to such existing towns as Peterborough and Northampton (28 in all are now designated). (See Fig. 15.) These will be supplemented in the future by substantial additions to some of the existing towns, and by very large new communities developed as the outcome of the regional strategy plans of the last decade which will be discussed later.

Related Development Controls

Although they are the most conspicuous parts of British planning, only a small part of total public sector activity is to be found in the new towns. Local authority public housing estates still provide half of all new housing for Britons. Private sector housing caters in large measure to families of at least middle class. Slum clearance has proceeded apace. Control of building licences (subsequently replaced by the requirement of planning permission to build), in combination with the development controls provided by the Act of 1947, provided for an effective public counterpoint to speculative profit-seeking private development through strict land use zoning principles. The 1947 Act made it obligatory for local authorities to control land use. Housing subsidies have encouraged higher density developments, both of apartments and offices. Industrial decentralisation has been substantial, although massive office growth has led to continued employment growth in central London. The Clean Air Acts have eliminated much of the smoky atmosphere of British towns. But Gordon Cherry (1972) argues that while the results have been impressive, they also have been surprisingly conservative :

The success of local authority intervention has been to see that development has occurred more or less at the right time in the right places. Schools have been built in accordance with housing programmes; open space has been reserved; building in certain areas has been restricted; elsewhere it has been encouraged; unfit houses have been demolished and new ones built; shopping centres rather than ribbons have been created; the worst excesses of badly sited industry have been avoided. This represents a high point in public

FIG. 15 Britain's new towns

intervention in the shaping of an urban environment. . . . A coherent strategy for the planned distribution of population and employment which was linked to a policy of containing the further growth of large cities was pursued. . . . But the total influence of planning intervention has to be seen in even wider terms than the security of order and a sense of rationality. Its greatest impact has been to bolster the traditional view of the West European city . . . that cities, as ancient repositories of culture, should be protected from decay. In this sense, planning has been essentially a conservative movement, aiming to retain traditional ideas about urban society and urban functions.

In other words, a nostalgic sense of attachment to urban forms, perceived to be functional in the past, has pervaded Britain's development controls.

The New Towns Assessed

If the development controls were conservative in their application, what of the radical alternative, the new towns? In many respects, London's new towns have been great successes, housing over 470,000 people. Peter Hall (1966) argues that they have become magnets for over 400 industrial plants, places of employment for over 250,000 workers, attractive shopping centres, and major market areas. But, in a deeper sense, they reflect a failure of Abercrombie's plan. The initial idea was to create self-contained communities that would receive a population of 400,000 and a corresponding amount of employment, developed by public corporations and acting as instruments for the removal of Londoners from a London prevented from growing and attracting jobs from outside.

The Abercrombie proposals were modified in several ways. Only eight new towns were designated instead of ten, and three of these were already well-established population centres. Many of the modifications were needed because Abercrombie's population forecasts proved to be in error. In the 1940s it was thought that the country faced a period of population stagnation. It was not expected that the population of the London region would increase, and plans for the early post-war period were concerned almost entirely with decentralisation, envisaging a movement of about one million people from the Greater London Conurbation to the Outer Metropolitan Area. The new towns were to play a major role in casting decentralisation into new forms.

Between 1951 and 1971 the Greater London Conurbation has,

indeed, decreased in population by some 3·0 per cent per decade. But the Outer Metropolitan Area has increased in population far more rapidly than this—between 1951 and 1961 alone by nearly the million envisaged as the 'ultimate' target in Abercrombie's plans. Thus, London's new towns had much less of a total impact on decentralisation than envisaged. By 1971 their population approached 470,000 people, with their ultimate targeted population 650,000, but this has represented only 18 per cent of population growth in the outer ring of South-eastern England.

The most important idea in the creation of the new towns was that they should be self-contained and balanced communities for working and living (Thomas, 1969), thus differing from the local authority housing estates, or private enterprise's version of the garden city, the commuting suburb attached to an existing settlement. Each new town was to be made up of neighbourhood units centring on schools, shops and other local facilities, following the concepts of Clarence Perry discussed earlier. The neighbourhoods, together with a major shopping centre, industrial estate, and a range of community-wide educational, cultural and recreational facilities, were to constitute a self-contained entity, with girdling open space. In this way the ideals of Ebenezer Howard would be met, combining the advantages of town and country with none of the disadvantages. Balance was to be achieved in several ways : between residence and employment, between facilities and needs, and also between social classes. For example, one of the charges to Lord Reith's committee in 1946 was as follows : 'If the community is to be truly balanced, so long as social classes exist, all must be represented in it . . . the community will be poorer if all are not there.' Thus, subsidised rental housing was to be provided alongside homes for higher income groups, and different family sizes and age groups would be catered for. It had been felt that, at Letchworth and Welwyn Garden City, a mixture of social classes had brought about a sense of community that was absent in most towns. It was hoped that a similar sense of community in which class distinctions were minimised could be created in the new towns by physical planning means. In most of the new towns, there was a mixture of housing for different groups in each neighbourhood.

The new towns have served as magnets for modern industry and have provided vastly improved physical conditions and housing for their residents, predominantly young Britons in the child-rearing stages of the family cycle. Slightly more than half of their residents came from London, but the Londoners tended to stay, for 96 per cent of the *net* immigration came from London (Thomas, 1969). For the others, the new towns acted as staging points in migration to parts of the country other than London.

In large measure the self-containment goal has been achieved. A far higher proportion of the residents of the new towns work in them than elsewhere, whereas in other parts of the Outer Metropolitan Zone of London, where population growth has been accommodated by the more conventional suburbs and housing estates, growth of car ownership and long-distance commuting to London have gone hand in hand. In the new towns, on the other hand, increasing entry of women into the labour force has increased rather than decreased their self-containment, and commuting to London has decreased.

The question of social balance in the new towns is much more debatable. A significant proportion of the residents in Harlow new town also had other family members in the town, frequently of the same generation, but also including retired parents because of the housing created for retirees. Critics have spoken of 'new town blues' of working-class families cut off from traditional social networks, of the increasing social homogeneity of towns from which professionals and managers move to private housing developed in surrounding villages. Yet studies comparing residents of new towns with those of old city boroughs have failed to find differences in psychosomatic or psychiatric symptoms attributable to the new environment (Pahl, 1970). To be sure, feelings of social isolation tended to be greater among those just separated by long distance from kin and friends, but they were soon offset by involvement in local circles. The greatest strains in the new towns appear to have been among the blue-collar workers displaced from inner-London neighbourhoods in which family and kinship ties were strongest (Young and Willmott, 1957). Where kin have moved to the same new town—in Harlow this was the case for 47 per cent of the families—these strains have been absent. And whereas there is a general feeling of satisfaction with the new community, there is little evidence that the life-style of the new town residents changed significantly as a result of the move. Nor is there any evidence in

Britain's class-conscious society that communications across class lines have improved.

It was possible to build socially mixed neighbourhoods in Letchworth and Welwyn Garden City *exactly because* the class system that pervaded inter-war Britain preserved social distances and specified the etiquette of social relationships across class boundaries. But in an increasingly mobile post-war society, the planners' ideal of the social mixing of housing has foundered. It had limited success in the early new towns because of the greater propensity of the middle class to move out to private housing estates adjacent to villages in surrounding areas. This led to stickiness in the market for the higher-priced dwellings. Thus, more recently, there has been a much greater degree of spatial segregation of housing types in the new towns. Social idealism has given way to the influences of the market (Heraud, 1968).

At the level of the towns as a whole, although they do have higher proportions of managers, professionals, and higher-skilled manual workers than the country as a whole—a consequence of their industrial structure—the new towns are far from the one-class communities that characterise North American suburbia. Instead, they have many neighbourhoods catering to the variety of housing needs of the persons employed in their industrial estates and commercial enterprises.

But now in Britain there are many calls for a shift in strategy. Thomas (1969) notes that the new towns

have ridden the crest of the wave. They have accommodated manufacturing industry . . . much originated from London. But manufacturing industry has been decentralising from London anyway. (They) have accommodated thousands of young mobile migrants from London. But so has the rest of the Outer Metropolitan Area. The fact that the new towns have moved with rather than against the tide has probably been the most vital ingredient in their successful growth.

Thomas, among others, calls for a new move with the newer tides of change in Britain.

New Trends and New Policies

London has continued to grow, and with rising real incomes and increased mobility, long-distance commuting is on the increase, creating commuting fields much like those in North America (Fig. 16).

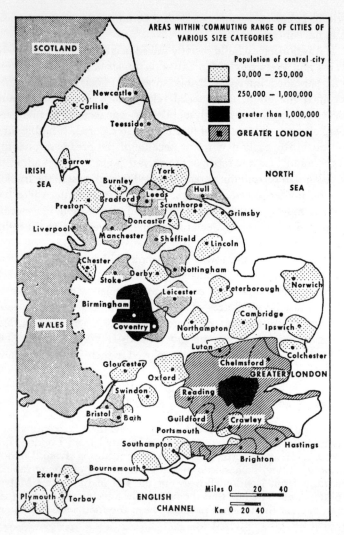

Fig. 16 Commuting fields of local authority areas in England in 1961

This map is adapted from the work of Peter Hall that in turn was modelled on the U.S. studies that resulted in Fig. 7.

Between 1961 and 1971, there was a consistent pattern of growth differentials favouring the outer rings of metropolitan areas in England and Wales. Of 52 meropolitan areas, 49 experienced relative decentralisation and, in 27 of them, central-area loss was coupled with outer-area growth to give absolute decentralisation (Kivell, 1972).

The basis of London's continued employment growth has been the office, not the factory. The 'office boom' of 1955–62, in particular, produced rapid increases in the number of jobs in central London, increasing congestion. Great concern about this resulted in growing pressure on the government to control office growth and engage in broader development strategies than those contained in the New Towns Policy (Cowan *et al.*, 1969). The government responded : a 1963 White Paper on Central Scotland suggested major expansion of East Kilbride, Cumbernauld, Livingston and Glen-Rothes into major growth zones, transforming the new towns into economic weapons to accelerate growth, reduce unemployment and change migration patterns. The South-East Study of 1964 and the later Strategic Plan for the South-East of 1970 recommended rethinking London's green belt strategy and the diversion of growth away from London to major new urban complexes near Southampton, at Crawley, around Reading, in South Essex, and at Northampton. These complexes, of at least 250,000 people, are regarded as weapons for spurring growth of the national economy and reducing the infra-structure costs of continued expansion of outer London.

The Strategic Plan for the South-East has been extended to other regions. The publication in September 1965 of a national economic plan up to 1970 led to the creation of the National Planning Council and of a regional planning council in each of the economic regions, each of which has produced its strategy studies. Thus, a policy originally aimed at controlling London's growth has been turned around to become a policy for national growth and development. The push to greater size and variety represents a new phase of new town planning in which traditional decentralisation and housing goals have been superseded by the attempt to use major new town developments as the leading edges of national growth policies. By developing those towns, the public has entered into a new role of developmental leadership, supplemented by the controls of the town and country planning machinery.

CONTINENTAL EUROPEAN DIRECTIONS

Such themes have been carried over to Continental Europe. Eben-ezer Howard's new towns philosophy and the successes of British planning have induced other countries to attempt to control physical development, to direct new settlement away from con-gested metropolitan centres, and to stimulate economic and urban growth in peripheral regions. The particular form of policy varies from country to country. For example, the French have been con-cerned for a decade and a half over the steady concentration of people and economic activity in Paris. The Finns have seen the population of the northern half of their country pour into Hel-sinki or leave Finland entirely. The Swedes are concerned because most of their people are concentrated in Stockholm and two other metropolitan areas of southern Sweden. They are not concerned because their metropolitan centres are too big, as the French are over Paris, but because the depopulation of the Swedish north threatens to erode the social structure in that section of their nation. The Hungarians share a similar concern over the domina-tion of their national economy by Budapest. Only the Poles are un-concerned with the outflow of rural people into their metropolitan areas. Lagging behind the rest of Europe in their rate of moderni-sation, the Poles see metropolitanisation as a process essential to absorb a 'surplus' rural population.

Despite these differences in forms, however, the central concern of urban policy in all of Europe is now the regional distribution of growth. Economic growth is viewed as the basic means to achieve social objectives such as improved income, housing, education, health, welfare, recreation, and so on. European growth policies are intended to ameliorate disparities in income and welfare be-tween regions of the country and, to a lesser extent, to minimise deleterious effects of economic growth on the natural environ-ment.

The goals and objectives of urban growth policies vary from country to country, but to some degree all are aimed at: (1) *balanced welfare*—achieving a more 'balanced' distribution of income and social well-being among the various regions of the country, as well as among social classes; (2) *centralisation/de-centralisation*—establishing a linked set of local and national public institutions which make it possible to develop, at the national level, overall growth strategies, integrated with regional or metropolitan planning and implementation that is partly a product of a reformed local governmental system and is directly accountable to local officials and the affected constituency; (3) *environmental protection*—channelling future growth away from areas suffering from environmental overload or which possess qualities worthy of special protection, towards areas where disruption of the environment can be minimised; (4) *metropolitan development*—promoting more satisfactory patterns of metropolitan development through new area-wide governmental bodies and the use of special land use controls, new towns, housing construction, new transportation systems, and tax incentives and disincentives; (5) *non-metropolitan development*—diverting growth into hitherto by-passed regions by developing 'growth centres' in presently non-metropolitan regions, constructing new transportation links between such regions and centres of economic activity, using various incentives and disincentives to encourage or compel location of economic activity in such areas, and forcibly relocating certain government activities into them.

Meanwhile, as attempts have been made to formulate these policies, many of the twentieth-century changes already described in North America and Britain have been unfolding in continental Europe, following emergence from the post-war period in which there had been preoccupation with reconstruction and meeting immediate housing shortages. But many of the changes have taken on distinctively European forms.

Between 1955 and 1970, employment in agriculture in the European Economic Community dropped from 24·3 to 13·4 per cent and, while manufacturing remained essentially stable, employment in the tertiary sector increased from 35·7 to 42·7 per cent (Elkins, 1973). Progressive concentration of population took place. At the same time, rising real incomes produced much greater automobile ownership, and the extension of commuting areas, as illustrated in the British case by Fig. 16, to cover much of the West European landscape. As we have already seen in Britain, the central city populations have tended to decline while metropolitan growth has been taking place.

But in spite of these apparent similarities, there are fundamental differences with the North American scene. Many industrial commuters live in rural villages, commute by bus or train, and frequently combine factory work with agricultural smallholdings—especially in Hessen, north-east Bavaria, Switzerland, south-west Germany, the Czech lands, parts of eastern France and the Low Countries. High proportions of white-collar workers, professionals and managers also commute by bus and train, for example throughout south-east England to London. Only where jobs are substantially decentralised do the higher status workers commute by automobile in large numbers.

The higher density of population in both rural districts and the closely built-up urban areas (Barcelona : up to 2000 per hectare; Naples : 1500 per hectare; Vienna : 750 per hectare) as compared with North American cities (26–65 per hectare) continues to provide the opportunity for solving movement problems by means of rapid transportation rather than by the automobile. In the sixties, big cities throughout Europe started subway construction (Rome, Milan, Vienna, Munich, Frankfurt-am-Main, Cologne, Hamburg, Stockholm, Madrid, Barcelona) and extensions (Paris). Fares are often kept lower than cost to enable the present 70 per cent of the continental European employees who travel to work by public transportation to continue to do so. In contrast to North America, in most European countries long-range traffic planning has, since the 1960s, become an integrated part of the master plans controlling urban growth patterns. And just as there is the preference in the European scene for public rather than private transportation, there remains the traditional preference for housing to be provided in the higher-density apartment complexes that are necessary to support mass transportation, rather than in single-family suburbs. Thus, whereas in North American metropolitan areas many traditional city centres have begun to rot away, throughout Europe public and private development are combining to preserve, rehabilitate and/or construct new city centres that continue to dominate urban life. One result is that many older central city neighbourhoods are going through a process of 'gentrification' as the affluent move back—a pattern which is occurring also in Canada and Australia, but which is limited in the American scene by problems of race to a few neighbourhoods that have been able, in the major metropolises such as Washington, D.C., and Chicago, to insulate themselves from the ghetto.

Thus as the Danish planner Steen Eiler Rasmussen has remarked, the cooperation of many circumstances has led to profoundly different urban patterns and expressions of need in Europe and between the European countries, and these have stamped themselves on national housing and town planning programmes. It is, therefore, appropriate to consider several different cases—Sweden, France and the Netherlands—to begin to appreciate the differing planning concepts and some of the consequences of this planning. Once again it bears repeating : we devote so much time to discussing planning in the European scene *because* it is one of the major twentieth-century human consequences of nineteenth-century industrial urbanisation.

Sweden's Achievements

Any such inquiry must begin with Sweden. In this country, high standards of living in a small, culturally homogeneous nation, combined with a strong central government committed to the principles of the welfare state, have provided the setting for forthright affirmative action. In the Stockholm area, in particular, public ownership of the land under development, and state control over the construction industry, have meant that plans, once approved, have been carried out as approved. Ninety to ninety-five per cent of the housing is built with government financial assistance, so the government determines the numbers and kinds of units that will be built each year. The planners have preferred large apartment buildings rather than single-family homes. The National Housing Board prescribes the standards of apartment construction, and has consistently maintained high architectural quality.

Not only is housing controlled. Land use is controlled; the ownership of land carries with it no inherent development rights. The Swedish government controls when and where urban development will occur. In this planning, several policy objectives have had priority : slowing the growth of Stockholm, Göteborg and Malmö; inducing industry to move into lagging regions; and maintaining economically sound smaller towns at sizes large enough to support adequate community services.

Achievement of the goals has been aided by the critical housing shortage and the control of land use. For several decades Sweden has had a chronic housing shortage, resulting in much doubling-up of families and substantial overcrowding. Simple availability of a home somewhere has over-ridden, for many Swedes, what might otherwise be their individual locational and housing preferences, which in large measure have been ignored by the planners. Once an apartment was made available to someone whose name had finally moved to the top of the waiting list, it would be taken regardless of other considerations. Private development is also subject to public control by the Master Plan, the function of which is to look ahead 15–20 years and to specify future locations for roads, water and sewerage lines, green belts and urban land use. Once accepted, uses contrary to its intentions are prohibited.

It is in this framework that the growth of Stockholm has been directed since the Second World War. Stockholm's planners were influenced in developing their plans of the desirable future city by Lewis Mumford, Clarence Stein, Patrick Abercrombie, and Clarence Perry—and in turn, therefore, by those who reacted against nineteenth-century industrial urbanisation. Satellite communities with adequate local facilities have been created, separated by green belts, and linked into an interdependent metropolitan whole of 1·5 million people by a public transportation system.

Although building began at Arsta in 1947 and Vällingby in 1950, the Master Plan for Stockholm dates from 1952, revised and modernised in 1966. It is a 'rolling plan' subject to 5-yearly revision, always looking ahead for 30 years, and it envisages a metropolitan region re-fashioned by building satellite communities located along transportation corridors radiating from the city centre, primarily rail and subway. Half of the labour force would be employed in the home community. Past decisions favoured the placing of development in differentiated nuclei along public transit corridors close to bodies of water. More recently, widespread car ownership and rising real incomes have dictated the addition of an extensive expressway network, the shift from neighbourhood to regional shopping centres and the provision of more housing options, as modifications of the traditional planning concept.

The key to successful planning was, first of all, extensive municipal ownership of land to be developed, largely purchased in the period 1900–30, but continuing, for example, to permit building of Sätra in the 1960s. Second, the public transport network was designed as the principal determinant of urban location and form, initially radiating from the city centre and expected to carry 75 per cent of all peak hour travel to and from central Stockholm.

Third, the satellite centres were built as unified developments. Vällingby, for example, was built neighbourhood by neighbourhood, outward from higher density structures surrounding a commercial core located above the principal subway station. Attractive architecture and careful blending with the physical landscape characterise the town, completed in 1954. Inside it, pedestrian and vehicular traffic are separated.

Reflecting rising real incomes, automobile ownership, and the new expressways, the next community to be completed (Farsta in 1960) has the same physical layout—tall apartments succeeded by lower slab apartment buildings, row houses, and then by limited numbers of single-family homes. But the shopping centre was built with a massive surrounding parking lot, and the size of residential units was increased. This trend to greater automobile use is reflected even more forthrightly in Skärholmen, now being built, and in the plans for Jarva. A greater variety of housing types is provided, and more low-profile homes.

In these plans Stockholm has provided an example of what forthright planning can achieve in changing the physical expression of urbanisation, and the conditions under which effective public controls can prevail, albeit in a small country with a relatively affluent and quite homogeneous population. The continuing source of conflict is that Sweden's planners prefer high-density housing concentrated near city centres and oriented to public transport, while increasingly affluent Swedes demand more low-density single-family homes and better facilities for the private automobile. As yet, Sweden has not found a way to contend effectively with the conflicts between the planners' ideals and the developing preferences of the citizenry in the planning process.

Finland: The Building of Tapiola

Finland shares all the urbanisation problems found elsewhere in Europe, but differs from Sweden in that the national government has not taken a forceful leadership role in urban development. Financial aid is provided for housing programmes, and, despite the fact that Finland has a long history of municipal land ownership, most construction is undertaken by private entrepreneurs. Master planning and zoning were only spelled out in the Building Law of 1958, and few plans have been completed.

In this framework, Helsinki has tried to develop a regional planning process. There is agreement that further concentrated growth of Helsinki should be stemmed. Thus, in contrast to the Stockholm plan for an integrated but spatially dispersed metropolis, Heikki von Hertzen developed the Seven Towns Plan. New communities are to be built, self-contained and independent, and separated by extensive green belts. Within the framework of the plan, the development is to be undertaken by private groups.

Tapiola is the first of the towns to be built by the Housing Federation, a coalition of welfare and trade organisations headed by von Hertzen. It is generally acknowledged to be an architectural masterpiece. Densities are low. Building styles are intermingled throughout the developed area. The public planners did not impose standards constraining the private designers, but instead gave them free rein. A radial expressway provides access to Helsinki. More than 90 per cent of the residents own their own houses or apartments.

Ann Louise Strong (1971) observes from the vantage point of a planner, that

Tapiola may be the most successful new community yet built. . . . People want to live there; they enjoy it. No group in Finnish society is foreclosed . . . and all groups pursue the possibility. Tapiola offers them humanity and convenience, modernity and comfort, urbanity and nature, people and tranquillity, taste and modest cost, variety and cohesion. It is a setting for the enhancement of man's spirit.

Yet other recent evaluations sound notes of caution. Tapiola is not self-contained, for jobs are unavailable there for half the population; more than half the population commutes to Helsinki. Further, Tapiola was developed to contain a proportional cross-section of Finnish society, and homes were built accordingly. But the design of the town has evoked such a popular response that under rising conditions of demand, prices have increased to exclude the poor, and Tapiola is becoming much more of a homogeneous middle-class suburb. Its very architectural success may thus signify its downfall as a social experiment.

France: Economic and Urban Planning Combine
In France a tradition of individualism has bred hostility towards governmental intervention to influence land use or capital investment. Against such a backdrop, a major national economic and

urban development planning effort has been launched. Following an immediate post-war focus on housing estates (*grands ensembles*), the major thrust of the national planning effort has been to industrialise underdeveloped peripheral regions, particularly in the southern and western portions of the country, to stimulate the growth of eight major metropoles, and to stem the growth of Paris.

French urban structure had, at the end of the Second World War, a distinctive continental flavour. Around the highly prized 16e Arrondissement in Paris, for example, the low mobility of working-class populations had built up the small social unit of the quarter, with its distinctive street life and tightly knit networks of kin-group and other social relationships. Many areas retained the floor-by-floor social distinctions noted much earlier by Kohl. These graded out to highly individualistic suburban areas with unplanned single-family housing in *pavillons*, or the development by the poor of teeming *bidonvilles*.

Policies of rent control, the Depression and the Second World War had created almost a complete gap in building in France for several decades. Combined with post-war migration and rising birth rates, a housing crisis of major proportions resulted, the effects of which can still be felt (Merlin, 1969). The immediate post-war response of the public authorities was to build the largest number of houses as quickly as possible, without regard to location, provision of amenities, or improvement of housing quality.

The only way in which the construction industry could cope with the problem was by building large numbers of standardised apartments using mass-production methods. Such was the basis of France's *grands ensembles*, which were also favoured by the planners on ideological grounds, as a departure from the excessive individualism and isolation of the *pavillons*, producing more collective forms of habitation which, by throwing residents of a variety of social origins together, would create a new classless society (Elkins, 1973).

By 1964, 200 such developments of at least 1000 dwellings each had been built, providing 365,000 apartment dwelling units (197,000 in the Paris region), largely for more youthful child-rearing families headed by salaried workers. Despite their planners' hopes, the *grands ensembles* have been much criticised for their monotony, lack of amenities and community spirit, denounced because of their overcrowding and the resulting deviant and delinquent behaviour, and said to be cold, impersonal, un-friendly and overpowering in scale. The French have coined the term *sarcellite* to describe the phenomenon, after the best-known *grand ensemble* in the Paris region. Yet they did help meet France's critical housing shortage.

While the focus in housing policy was on the *grands ensembles*, there was growing concern with the problems of Paris. At present, nearly 20 per cent of the country's population lives in the Paris area, which also accounts for 50 per cent of the country's business turnover, 33 per cent of the country's college students, 65 per cent of its artists and writers, and 54 per cent of its publishing activity. In the Paris area is 50 per cent of the electrical construction indus-try, 56 per cent of the aircraft industry, 64 per cent of the auto-mobile industry, and 76 per cent of the pharmaceutical industry. On the other hand, there are only three other centres in the coun-try with a population of over 500,000 (Marseille, Lyon, and Lille–Roubaix–Tourcoing complex).

Two streams of policy developed, one focusing on the transfor-mation of the Paris region into a decentralised metropolis, the other on creating major new growth centres elsewhere in France.

The history of these efforts is of interest. Even after the Second World War France had very limited planning tools. Yet new intel-lectual currents were beginning to appear in a country which had very conservative cultural and political traditions and a highly centralised administration. In 1947, a young geographer called Jean-François Gravier wrote a book entitled *Paris et le désert français* that attracted wide attention with its diagnosis of nation-al ills relating to the imbalance of Paris's dominance, and its re-commendations that a policy of decentralisation be developed. Out of the debate that ensued emerged a progressive elaboration of planning tools, the 1958 Plan d'Aménagement et d'Organisa-tion Générale de la Région Parisienne (PADOG), and the Nation-al Urban Growth Strategy focusing on the *métropoles d'équilibre*.

PADOG's initial strategy was to try to halt the physical growth of Paris, reducing congestion at the centre by massive improve-ment in transportation infra-structure, and by diverting growth to major new nodes in the suburbs. The plan specifically rejected the British green belt and new towns ideas, however; the new urban nuclei were to be linked to the core by a system of expressways. It quickly became apparent that PADOG's estimate of one million new inhabitants during the sixties was too conservative, and it was replaced in 1965 by the *Schéma directeur*, the Strategic Plan for the District of Paris. This plan views the creation of new urban centres as the only remedy for the underequipment of the suburbs and the overcongestion of the centre. To assure an adequate amount of land for construction and green space, sites must be on the fringe of the present agglomeration. Growth of population will be channelled along 'preferential axes' chosen to fit the physical, economic, and human geography of the region. The principal axis will move downstream along the Seine, a direction in which growth is already relatively rapid, toward the Norman agglomerations of Rouen and Le Havre, which together comprise the second port of France. Along this axis, new communities are being created which will contain a full range of urban facilities and can accommodate from 300,000 to 1,000,000 inhabitants each. Specifically, these new communities are to be located tangential to the Paris core on a north-west–south-east alignment from Noisy le Grand to Cergy-Pontoise (which is now being built) and Tigery-Lieusaint to Mantes. In all, eight new communities are envisioned by the year 2000, five to the south and three to the north of the Seine, with six urban centres in the inner ring around Paris to be renovated, including Choisy-le-Roi-Rungis, where a new national food market has been built to replace Les Halles. Thus the new scheme will break with the radial-concentric pattern which has heretofore contributed to the region's difficulties. Transportation facilities will be provided to link the new towns with one another as well as with Paris, but one of the main aims of the new towns will be to provide self-sufficient communities where people can live and work without having to make long trips.

Complementing the *Schéma directeur* for the Paris region is the National Urban Growth Strategy, developed especially during the fifth plan of 1966–9. The basic idea of this strategy came from the work of other French geographers: Pierre George, who argued that whereas in the past regions made cities, today cities make regions; and J. Hautreux and M. Rochefort, whose book *La Fonction Régionale dans l'Armature Urbaine Française* (1964) identified eight metropolitan areas whose growth could offset the dominance of Paris. Thus, the urban strategy plans give high priority to public incentives to spur growth in Lyon–St-Étienne,

Marseille–Aix, Lille–Roubaix–Tourcoing, Toulouse, Nancy–Metz, Bourdeaux, Nantes–St-Nazaire, and Strasbourg.

The mechanisms to achieve the goals of the *Schéma directeur* and the *métropoles d'équilibre* are, first of all, the succession of national economic plans, combined with a national land use plan. These plans have, in turn, been regionalised as part of the search for a 'better' distribution of population that reflects not simply economic purposes, but more balanced development and more equitable well-being. Local communities are expected to have comprehensive plans consistent with regional objectives. Six OREAM (Organisateurs d'Études d'Aménagement d'Aires Metropolitaine) have been established by the metropolitan areas of Marseille, Lyon–St Étienne, Metz–Nancy, the North, the lower Seine and the lower Loire, to trace long-term development prospects and urban planning needs, taking the year 2000 as a planning horizon. The principal local controls on land use involve the designation of priority zones of urbanisation (ZUPs) and deferred development zones (ZADs). These zones are specified by the municipalities, subject to national approval. Once a ZUP is approved, national funding for land acquisition and the government's 30–50 per cent contribution for streets, 40 per cent for sewerage, and 25 per cent for water supply is directed there and withheld from ZADs. Government funding is also available to aid housing construction. Various tax incentives can also be used to induce development in desired directions.

The *Schéma directeur* calls for new towns within the Paris Basin, as we have described earlier (Merlin, 1969). It is a plan that is much criticised by those who fear that limited funds will be diverted from the regional decentralisation plans to the construction of massive new towns in the Paris Basin that will, admittedly, reshape and decentralise the metropolitan region, but divert investment back from the provinces towards this re-fashioning of the metropolis. Thus, the *Schéma directeur* and the *métropoles d'équilibre* have assumed a competitive rather than the complementary relationship they were intended to have.

The *Schéma directeur* reflects the spread of British thinking, even though the British new towns form was disavowed. Yet France has also produced a variety of dramatic new alternative plans for urbanisation, too, as we noted earlier when we discussed Le Corbusier's *Ville Radieuse*. The outstanding recent French idea in urban development that follows Corbusier is the *Cité Parallel*. The spiny backbone style of this idea is best expressed at Le Mirail, near Toulouse. This is a new 100,000-inhabitant community, designed by Georges Candilis and intended to serve the aerospace complex the government is creating in the Toulouse area. It will have green areas larger than Paris's Bois de Boulogne and Bois de Vincennes combined and will provide separate streets for pedestrians and cars. 72 per cent of the people will be housed in 5–14-storey flats and another 16 per cent in 2–4-storey flats. It represents a distinctively European alternative design concept to that of the British new towns.

The Netherlands: Focus on the Human Consequences of Urbanisation

Yet other plans are being formulated and executed in the Netherlands, one of the most urbanised countries in the world, but without a city of over one million population. Much of its population lives in physically separate medium-size cities situated in a horseshoe pattern around a relatively open agricultural heart in the eastern part of the country. This horseshoe development is referred to as the 'Randstad'. Travel between any two points in the area does not require much more than one hour. There is considerable commuting, yet each city is differentiated enough to provide a variety of jobs and facilities. So far, planning for the area has sought to maintain this arrangement by stimulating growth in other parts of the country, preserving open space, creating new towns on new land claimed from the sea, and improving the inter-urban transportation system. Thus, it is hoped that the present multiple-nuclei, dispersed urbanisation pattern will continue to prevail, and that the green heart of Randstad can be preserved.

Amenity is the national government's basic reason for seeking to limit metropolitan growth. No other national government demonstrates quite the same concern for the social consequences of urbanisation. The concern encompasses the preservation of a choice among living environments, and protection of individuality. Retention of Randstad's green core and city separators is a major national goal. Yet, in contrast, Rotterdam takes a view contrary to that of the national government, seeking growth in the belief that it is necessary to remain competitive in a united Europe.

Control of Randstad is being sought after in several ways, in the face of continuing pressures to develop the green heart in the interests of growth. Emigration is a national goal. Both physical and economic planning are undertaken at the national level. After remarkable post-war accomplishments in restoring a devastated housing stock, sparked by government subsidy programmes, the Netherlands thus embarked upon a policy of polycentric 'concentrated deconcentration', based on the realisation of environmental goals. People would be encouraged to settle in four multi-nuclear urban zones. Demands for lower-density single-family housing were acknowledged, but strict developmental controls applied to avoid sprawl. The actual planning has had three ingredients : direct investment in roads, infra-structure, schools, etc., inducing private investment; plan enforcement, determining development in designated green spaces; and incentives for developing problem areas. Growth in Randstad is to be outwards along transport routes, separated by agricultural buffer zones, preserving both the historic cities and the agricultural heart.

In contrast to other parts of Randstad, Rotterdam has experienced rapid growth, and represents an outstanding example of post-war central city redevelopment (its Lijnbaan is a prototype copied by shopping centre developers throughout the world), new port development—Europort, and the use of municipal land acquisition to permit satellite city development both to stem the growth of the central city and to control the pattern of suburbanisation.

The latter perhaps is the most significant difference emerging in the urbanisation process between Western Europe and North America : public creation of satellite communities, with consistent overall architectural design, green belts and open space, specification of growth directions, and clear preferences for mass transportation, as opposed to private development of automobile-oriented suburbs drifting after major style-setting, profit-seeking private initiatives.

THE CITY OF SOCIALIST MAN

The Communist Revolution of 1917 marked the beginning in Russia, and later in eastern Europe, of yet another path in urban development. The revolutionaries had great faith in the power of the government to transform society for the betterment of man, in seizing the government not to restrict its power but rather to use it. They aspired to remould society through a state monopoly of the production of goods, of means of communications, of education, and of science.

The great modernising revolutions that took place much earlier in the west and at a more leisurely pace of gradual transition came concurrently in the Soviet Union and took a more dramatic and radical form. The religious revolution, which in the west found expression in the Reformation, the Counter-Reformation and the gradual secularisation of most aspects of life, took the form in the Soviet Union of militant atheism. The economic revolution, which as the Industrial Revolution in the west extended over more than a century, took the form in the Soviet Union of state ownership and management of the entire economy to promote social goals and to speed industrialisation. The democratic political revolution, which found expression in the west in the American and French revolutions and the gradual diffusion of political power in Britain through a series of reforms, in the Soviet Union took the form of transfer of power from the autocracy of the Tsars to the dictatorship of the proletariat through the leadership of the Communist party with centralised authority but democratic participation. The intellectual revolution, which in the west flowered in the Age of Reason or the Die Aufklärung and in which faith developed in the perfectibility of man and social institutions, in the ability of man by rational thought and scientific investigation to improve himself and society and to rule the universe, in the Communist Revolution took the form of an optimistic faith in the ability of the Party and the Government, through science and industrialisation, to transform society and social relations and to create a rational communistic world order.

The Soviet Experience

What was sought in urban development was what Lenin had called 'a new pattern of settlement for mankind', the city of socialist man. The classic writings of Marxism–Leninism suggested ways in which the goal might be achieved : planning was to create cities without social or economic divisions; there was to be a commitment to the socially integrative value of housing and a wide range of social services; city planning was to be responsive to economic planning, which would determine industrial location and set limits to the rate of urbanisation in developed regions and major urban complexes; and thus city planning *per se* was to be restricted to a basic physical-engineering-architectural profession, providing high-density new developments in approved styles.

The accomplishments of the Soviets in urban development are unquestionable. During the Soviet period the U.S.S.R. has been transformed from a rural society to a predominantly urban one, through a combined process of industrialisation and urbanisation achieved as the outcome of a series of five-year plans. The population was 82 per cent rural in 1926, but 56 per cent urban in 1969, at which time the U.S.S.R. had 209 cities of more than 100,000 people. Chauncy D. Harris (1970) has revealed several things about the urban system that has been created. First, size and economic power within the urban network are closely related; each of 24 major urban regions has a relatively complete urban hierarchy that corresponds with the administrative hierarchy of the 'command' economy. Second, growth has been led by economic policies, while the succession of economic plans has brought this growth and its associated urbanisation to regions successively more remote from Moscow.

Other conditions have also affected the urban development process, particularly after the Second World War : wartime devastation and the high cost of bringing existing cities up to minimal standards; the political rigidity of the Stalinist era, its single-minded focus on specified planning standards, and its peculiar baroque architectural manifestations; the necessity to develop basic industrialised construction skills, emphasising quantity rather than quality; the basic emphasis on heavy industry in investment allocations, with only small percentages going to housing, urban development and service facilities.

The authoritarian role of the central government and the priority of the economic goals of the state have been expressed at all levels of urbanisation, down to the precise physical nature of the new urban developments that have been built. The procedure is as follows. The State Planning Commission determines the economic norms for the city and, therefore, the basic employment required. Given this basic employment figure as a base, the city planner's role is simply to implement existing norms, also determined by the central planning authorities and laid out in basic books of standards : *Regulations and Norms for the Planning and Construction of Cities: USSR* (translated by the U.S. Joint Publications Research Service [*Pravilia i Normy Planirovki i Zastroyki Gorodov*], Moscow, 1959, and *Handbook for Designers: City Planning* [*Spravocnik proetirorshika-gradostroitelstvo*], *Moscow*, 1963. These books lay out the physical layout, densities, street patterns, utilities networks, and so on, of the settlements to be built (Fisher, 1962). Building proceeds in the Soviet Union on the basis of *microrayons* (neighbourhood units), built for 6000–12,000 people together with whatever services are specified for inclusion in them.

The automatic nature of the process is both a result of the directed nature of the Soviet state, and the need to provide massive quantities of housing and urban services after years of neglect of urban needs, as a result of preoccupation with industrialisation and the long period for which the effects of wartime devastation were felt. A major goal of standardisation was to industrialise housing construction through factory production of prefabricated and precast materials and forms, both to reduce costs and speed construction to meet the immense needs for housing. Since quantity was so important, quality was sacrificed, and nowhere does one find more drab and monotonous modern cities, and buildings with poorer internal design, than in the U.S.S.R., although there are attempts today to provide a greater range of building styles, apartment sizes, and qualities of developments. The industrialised methods produce standard apartment blocks almost exclusively. Movement in the cities is by public transportation. Services and facilities are the minimum necessary. An elaborate, often monumental, political-cultural administrative core is provided for the city, surrounded by a succession of self-contained neighbourhood units, undifferentiated socially.

The individual city plans, as in the case of Moscow, nonetheless have a distinctive new town flavour. Official Soviet policy is to restrain Moscow's growth and to channel such outlying growth as occurs into satellite towns. Like Abercrombie's Greater London Plan, that for Moscow is formulated in a series of rings. Within the inner belt highway, growth will be restrained. Focus will be on major rehousing schemes, facilitated by industrialisation of a standardised housing industry. This is encircled by a green belt, a 10-kilometre wide ring being developed into a recreation area, in which residential dacha construction is being restrained.

Finally, there are the satellite towns (*goroda–sputnika*), accommodating new growth, and built according to the standardised *microrayon* physical design specifications outlined earlier.

The resulting spatial patterns are held to be consistent with socialist principles of urban development, the antithesis of the European industrial urbanisation of the nineteenth century that so angered and repelled Marx and Engels. One Polish planner's version of the principles is as follows (Fisher, 1962) : the principles of social justice are realised by using the official norms and standards which determine per capita living spaces, population density, and quantity of services adjusted to projected population limits without class distinctions. The only basis for differentiation of available environment among urban families are the biological characteristics of the families. Functional and spatial structure of new residential areas and towns corresponds, due to the development of functionally similar neighbourhood units and to the social conception of a socialist urban community.

The Impact of Russian Socialism on Eastern Europe's Cities

These principles have been applied throughout Eastern Europe since the Second World War, although distinctively different styles of urban development are distinguishable : (1) the post-war reconstruction period, when (with the exception of the meticulous reconstruction of Warsaw as it had existed in 1939, as Poland's national symbol) housing was to be built as quickly as possible; (2) a period of 'Stalinesque' massive developments; and (3) the 'post-Stalin modern' period.

During the Stalinist period, there was a strong ideological overtone that the socialist city should be significantly different from that of the West, and uniform in its characteristics, consistent with the goal of social equality. Eastern European planning at that time showed heavy Soviet influence, and there was consistent application of Soviet procedures, norms and plans. The buildings that were constructed were massive and the town planning 'absolutist baroque', typified by the Stalin Allee in East Berlin, or North Avenue in Bucharest, along which the Open Air Museum of Folklore and the Academy of Sciences greet visitors. In this period, too, were started some of the socialist new towns, designed to represent complete departures from western experience. Many are showplaces of the new socialist city : Nowa Huta in Poland, Dunaujvaros in

Hungary, Titograd in Yugoslavia, to mention a few. The cities accomplish a specific economic purpose—to house steelmill workers, or those in a regional administrative centre. Their form is simple : a square of administrative-cultural composition at the centre, with radiating streets flanked by massive residential developments comprising 5–9-storey apartment buildings containing 2–3-room apartments for families, and dormitories for unmarried workers. Adjacent to the complex is the economic unit that provides the employment.

In this period, too, the application of Socialist principles to existing cities began to have a significant impact on their spatial form and social structure.

For example, the effect of Russian-style socialism on the cities of East Germany, differentiating them from their counterparts of the west, has been to reduce areal specialisation and segregation by substituting for market processes direct planning by the state (Elkins, 1973). The expansion of the central office-shopping core has ceased and the type of retailing has changed. Land vacated by departing industry has been occupied by apartment blocks, and people have been brought back to the central city. The high prestige assigned to manufacturing industry has resulted in the dispersion throughout the city of large industrial complexes with associated housing areas. Because new residential development is all in apartments, significant density differences among parts of the city have been ironed out, and social segregation has been largely abolished. Housing policy is to give priority in new dwellings to young families with children, employees in key jobs, and families living in bad conditions. Thus, there is a strong correlation between age of structures and age of inhabitants, producing socially mixed neighbourhoods with the virtual disappearance of social status as a differentiating factor. Only intellectuals and party leaders enjoy a distinctive residential area. And because there is little reliance on the automobile, all residential areas are closely related to public transportation facilities. Similar changes are reported throughout Eastern Europe.

Since Stalin greater variety in building styles has emerged, however, and the planning process and goals have come to differ from one country to another. The philosophic tenets of Marxist–Leninist dogma and their implications for operational city planning are being re-examined, but several features do stand out and persist : standardisation; concern for the proper size of cities; a particular concept of the city centre; and development by neighbourhood units (Fisher, 1962).

But the nature of these concerns has begun to diverge. Only where the scale of construction has been great enough has prefabricated construction proved to be economical, in the major cities of Poland, Hungary, and Czechoslovakia. Elsewhere, there has been greater reliance on traditional building techniques. And although apartment houses and tenements were nationalised throughout Eastern Europe, this is still not the case everywhere with urban land, much of which remains in private ownership, albeit strictly controlled by zoning and subject to alienation for public purposes. In Hungary, for example, each year a considerable amount of public land is divided into lots and sold by the government for construction of condominiums, single-family housing and weekend homes, and in Budapest this is producing a certain amount of social differentiation between the elite neighbourhoods to the west in old Buda and the working-class communities of old Pest to the east.

Most eastern European planners are seeking to create city centres with other than the monumental and political-administrative functions of the Stalinesque baroque. While all agree on the necessity for neighbourhood unit development, they differ on the nature of these units. Finally, in all countries there is concern for the 'proper' or 'balanced' size of city based on the primary economic functions of the place, and in all cases there is the underlying conviction that large cities must have their growth contained, and that new towns and satellite cities should be built around large urban agglomerations.

The Continuing Debate About Urban Goals

Throughout Eastern Europe, therefore, the traditional western debate that ultimately led to western Europe's new towns policies has been joined, and the role of ideology in the selection of an urban future once more comes to the fore. More clearly than anywhere else, in the socialist societies what men believe determines the future they try to create, but one sees in the Soviet literature today major debates about the desired urban future.

One such widely publicised debate is between two scholars influential in the Soviet planning process, geographer B. S. Khorev

(1972) and economist V. V. Perevedentsev (1972). Khorev argues that continued attempts must be made in the Soviet Union to develop new forms of urbanisation consistent with the tenets of Marxism–Leninism. He writes that the division of labour leads in the first place to a separation of industrial and commercial labour from the labour of agriculture and, thus, to a separation of town from countryside. In a class society this separation produces antagonism between town and countryside. But as classes disappear and society is rebuilt on a communist foundation, he feels that significant differences between town and countryside also gradually disappear.

The essence of long-range changes in settlement and in growth of cities lies in the gradual erasing of differences between town and countryside, to yield a unified system of settlement, whose planned regulation may help prevent haphazard and uncontrolled city growth.

The classic writings of Marxism–Leninism, according to Khorev, suggest ways of achieving that goal : harmonious development of productive forces according to a single plan; a more uniform distribution of large-scale industry and population throughout the country; achievement of close internal links between industrial and agricultural production; expansion of the means of transportation; reduction of the concentration of population in large cities. To date, he argues,

we have experienced a concentration of industrial production and urban population. Revolutionary changes are now leading to a single system of settlement, a functionally delimited and structurally interrelated network of places that can be regulated in a planned manner for the benefit of society, and encompassed by a unified system of regional planning, a type of spatial organisation that can be conceived only as an integral combination of artificial and natural environments.

Perevedentsev contests this argument saying that the literature on city planning is strewn with expressions like excessive growth, excessive development, excessive concentration, excessive saturation with industry. 'I once made persistent efforts to find out what the originators of such expressions had in mind. Alas, I did not succeed in determining this. Here, everything is excessive.' He notes that B. S. Khorev writes : 'The excessive, hypertrophic growth of our large and superlarge cities is inexpedient and undesirable.' Perevedentsev asks, 'Where do the hypertrophy and excessiveness start? At what size?' 'One searches in vain', he says, 'for the criteria of optimal size or of excessiveness', noting that the productivity of social labour is generally considered to be the chief criterion for effectiveness in distributing production forces. Calculations show that the productivity of labour in large cities is many times higher than that in the small ones, and in the superlarge cities it is many times higher than in the large cities. Thus, for example, the productivity of labour in the industry of cities with populations of more than 1,000,000 persons is 38 per cent higher than in cities with populations of from 100,000 to 200,000 and the return on assets is more than twice as high.

Perevedentsev also notes the ineffectiveness of attempts to limit growth by registration requirements placed on migrants. 'Many large cities have long had rigidly limited registration; they grow and grow all the same.' By no means is the problem here attributable to natural growth (the preponderance of births over deaths), which in the largest cities is insignificant. In Moscow, for example, in 1967 it was 1·7 persons for every 1000 residents—that is, 11,000 for all of Moscow—but Moscow's annual growth still amounted to more than 60,000. The administrative regulation of migration has proved ineffective in the extreme, and where there has been some success it has led only to a shortage of manpower—that is, industry and other branches of the national economy were unable to exploit their potentialities. The manpower shortage in many cities has only been alleviated by increasing the number of people who commute to work every day from the suburbs. The price is high. Many commuters spend an hour and a half or two hours en route, in addition to the usual city norm, and some spend even more. They commute to work in Moscow from as far as 100 km or more away.

What Perevedentsev sees in the Soviet Union is continued population concentration in major cities in the foreseeable future, because major structural shifts are taking place in the national economy. The proportion of people employed in the 'primary' sphere—in agriculture and extractive industry—is growing smaller. The proportion of people employed in the manufacturing and the service industries is growing. But extractive industry is the industry of small cities, whereas manufacturing industry is the industry of large cities. Economic reforms promoting greater efficiency in industrial production will contribute to the trend. The increased effectiveness of enterprises situated in the large cities will inevitably promote a tendency toward priority development of them. And, of course, in the majority of cases, the reconstruction of enterprises is considerably more advantageous than the construction of new ones. Further, since science holds first place in the rate of increase of employees, its share in the economy will increase rapidly. And in Soviet conditions science is a big city industry. Finally, the entire service sphere, which lags behind the other branches of the national economy, is inevitably bound to those places where people are concentrated. Its importance for the growth of cities will increase more and more. Social factors will play an increasing role, too. The large city will become increasingly more attractive as people's free time increases. The importance of contacts made outside work will grow, and the conditions for this in a small city simply cannot be compared to those in a well-organised large city. Thus, the state policy of regulating the growth of cities must be based on a precise knowledge of the relative shortcomings and advantages of cities of various sizes and types. To do this it is necessary to study the economic, social, demographic, public health and other aspects of the growth of cities. Right now, he says that knowledge of these factors is patently inadequate, and what is known speaks in favour of large cities rather than against them. In the U.S.S.R., apparently, continuing centralisation is most likely, at the time that planned decentralisation is changing urban areas in Western Europe.

5 Divergent Paths in Twentieth-Century Urbanisation

PERHAPS the most widely held thesis of recent decades about the social consequences of urbanisation is that of the convergence of social forms. Sjoberg (1965), one of the leading proponents of this view, writes that

industrial cities over the world are becoming alike in many aspects of their social structure . . . as technology becomes increasingly complex, a significant number of structural imperatives become more narrowly defined. . . . Modern technology . . . encompasses scientific know-how. In turn, the scientific method seems to support and is itself sustained by an ideology that gives rise to and promotes the democratic process, and such norms as universalism and emphasis on achievement in modern bureaucracies.

There was a logic to the arrangement of the preceding chapters in a spectrum of urbanisation experiences from those obtaining under conditions of laissez-faire privatism to the highly centralised circumstances of the socialist states that argues strongly for a contrary view. Modernism has *not* meant the westernism of conventional wisdom, the Wirthian theory of the human consequences of urbanisation with which we began, for Wirth's theory was found to be both time and culture-bound to the immigrant city of the nineteenth century. In twentieth-century North America different social theories were found to be needed to account for the consequences of urbanisation. Equally different concepts will be needed in the Third World to provide a basis for comprehending contemporary urban dynamics in nations with widely varying cultures, where new governments are beginning to try to control urbanisation and to cast it into forms held to be more desirable than those thought likely to result from unconstrained urban growth, often for reasons of social and economic equity. Effective planning for such purposes was found increasingly to be the hallmark of the redistributive welfare states of Western Europe, where it was seen that urban growth has been cast into new physical forms commensurate with the utopian constructs of Ebenezer Howard and Le Corbusier. Finally, the control of urbanisation was shown to reach its maximum in the centralised command economies of the socialist states, where planning for the city of socialist man has been undertaken in circumstances in which status and neighbourhood differences have been reduced, and where continuing housing shortages eliminate the freedom of individual choice.

THE SOCIO-POLITICAL BASES

A sequence of socio-political forms is suggested, arranged along a spectrum in which there is increasing public involvement in deliberately managing urbanisation to produce social consequences other than those conventionally perceived to result from the increasing size, density and heterogeneity of urban population concentrations. Indeed, perhaps the most important of the human consequences of urbanisation during the twentieth century may well be this attempt to change the nature of its perceived nineteenth-century consequences, to produce by coercive means more humane urban environments. Looking forward, urbanisation processes will, in the next decades, be similarly contrived in more parts of the world than today. Even where central controls do not prevail, substantial pressures will exist for governments to move into the policy arena to alter urban futures. As Lloyd Rodwin (1970) has remarked, 'Before World War II almost no one wanted the central government to determine how cities should grow. Today, only a generation later, national governments throughout the world are adopting or being implored to adopt urban growth strategies.' Moreover, he concludes that 'radical changes in technology and in analytical and planning methods may make significant changes in the urban system not only feasible, but to some extent manipulable'. The diverse forms that public intervention is taking, the variety of goals being sought, and the differences in manipulation and manipulability from one society to another are combining to produce increasingly divergent paths of deliberate urbanisation. This makes it all the more important to understand the relations between socio-political forms and urbanisation, because the socio-polity determines the public planning style. Urbanisation, in this sense, can only be understood within the broad spectrum of closely interrelated cultural processes; among these processes, planning increases rather than decreases the range of social choice as modernisation takes place, while simultaneously restricting the range of individual choice to conform to the social path selected.

Free Enterprise Dynamics

At one extreme of the spectrum is the free enterprise, decentralised, market-directed system. In such societies decisions are made by individuals, and groups of decisions interact in the market through the free interplay of the forces of demand and supply. Economic and political power, vested in the claims of ownership and property, is widely dispersed and competitively exercised. The instruments of collective or government action are used only to protect and support the central institutions of the market and to maintain the required dispersion of power. Such is the classical nineteenth-century model which remains the underpinning today in the United States, Canada and Australia.

Success in the competitive system delivers status and power, which in turn enable the successful to determine the course of urbanisation by their choices, because others in society ape them. Power, of course, means control of the political system, and this power is exercised to protect property rights in the private land market and to preserve both the fruits of success and the competitive system in which it was achieved. The public role is limited to combating crises that threaten the societal mainstream as privately initiated innovation produces social change. Legal systems are mainly regulatory, too, functioning to preserve established values; indeed, the reliance of American law upon the regulatory approach to city building has meant the atrophy of city planning as a constructive element in social change (Warner, 1972). Planning practice has clearly been ineffectual in confronting the tremendous conflicts inherent in such undertakings as the building of the national Interstate Highway System and other major public works ventures undertaken by public agencies, yet delivering their rewards to private interest groups. No success whatever has been achieved in ameliorating poverty. The poor performance of the public sector in both the United States and Canada is, in this regard, a function both of the free-enterprise ideology and of the fragmented governments which the ideology maintains, together with fiscal systems that allocate tasks without resources to city governments.

The crux of it all is clearly the desire to maintain open competition. In the United States the benefits of redistributive welfare systems, mass public housing and rationalised urban investment inherent, for example, in European socialism have been eschewed in favour of unshakeable commitment to the private land and labour markets. Where there are differences between what is happening to cities in the United States on the one hand, and Canada and Australia on the other, they are to be found in the deep-seated white racism that exists as an additional feature of American culture, rather than in any differential pattern of rewards flowing from the commitment to competitive private lives.

Organisational Market Negotiation

As was noted in Chapter 2, increasing organisational scale and concentration of power is a dominant characteristic of today's new industrial and post-industrial states. As the scale of economic and bureaucratic organisation increases, changes arise in the dynamics of social and economic change. Major developmental decisions are made by negotiation among large-scale autonomous organisations and by voluntary associations, profit-oriented but not necessarily maximisers, countervailing and countervailed against, negotiating together and existing in a context of negotiated relationships, rather than delivered by the guiding hand of the market. Power is determined as a matter of policy or agreed upon by counterbalancing powers. Under such conditions there is organisation of production by large corporations run for the benefit of stockholders, while labour negotiates wages through large-scale unions. The consumption of end products is partly determined by individual choice, and partly by governmental policy. The collective power of organisations, collective power of the government, and the free choice of individuals are all part of the system. Hence, the 'market' is no longer the single master. Rather, elaborate negotiation for 'satisfactory' solutions tends to prevail; instead of maximisation, there is 'satisficing' and, increasingly, each of the large-scale organisations engages in planning in terms of corporate goals, often with systems analysis staffs at their disposal to help them select desirable courses of action.

Under such conditions, the public can begin to play an assertive countervailing or leadership role in urbanisation. Thus, while the approach to urban growth which prevailed in many Australian cities until recently seems to have been to allow random, unplanned development and to let such development take place simply in accordance with the fluctuations of the real estate market, increasing dissatisfaction with the laissez-faire city is now being expressed. For example, the State of Victoria now has a Decentralisation Minister, who is calling for directed decentralisation of half a million people from Melbourne into outlying country centres by the year 2000. Also, the Town and Country Planning Board of Victoria issued a *Report on Organisation for Strategic Planning* in which it stated that the four broad components for strategic planning and programming should be those of the pattern of urban land use for future growth, the pattern of rural–urban land conversion, the transport system and the utilities system. What is envisaged is control of urban growth via the supply of basic public works and services on the one hand, and development consents on the other, since both are necessary prerequisites for private action. Private housing and industrial development, the report says, can and should be steered by affirmative programming of basic infra-structural provision such as railway lines, highways, gas, electricity, telecommunications, water, sewerage, main drainage, schools, hospitals, and so on.

This idea of the public counterpoint in the development process has been taken one step further in both France and Japan. The French case was discussed in Chapter 4. In the instance of Japan, accelerated post-war laissez-faire centralisation of population and economic activity has taken place. Up to the end of the Second World War Japan had been a highly centralised state. The nationalism that had been the basis of Japanese development policies since the beginnings of modernisation in the Meiji era also conferred other powers, in particular the capacity to direct industrial decentralisation and to hold in check migration to the major cities. The nationalist doctrine underwent great change after Japan's defeat in the Pacific War, however, as the Occupation Forces' policies sought to eliminate it as a driving force in Japanese life and to replace it by the American model of a decentralised democratic power structure containing competing interest groups. This had disastrous effects in the cities, many Japanese now think, for central government controls were eliminated in favour of political decentralisation. This, in turn, permitted accelerated *centralisation* of population and economic activity, as part of the drive for economic growth that sacrificed both public and private consumption to further capital formation. Major developmental problems that had been held in check in earlier times resulted, including land scarcity and environmental pollution.

At the end of the Second World War Japan's large cities were devastated. In Tokyo 768,000 homes (56 per cent of the housing stock) had been destroyed and 51 per cent of the population were homeless. But Tokyo recovered faster than any other city in Japan following the war, and this led to massive immigration from other devastated areas. Many of the city's slums had their origin at this time, in spite of the fact that 1·5 million housing units were created between 1945 and 1964, three-quarters built by private enterprise. Seiichi Yasui, then Governor of Tokyo, successfully took the lead in developing special legislation for the city under the National Capital Regional Development Law of 1956. Under its provisions, integrated plans for 'regulating' and 'readjusting' the growing population of Tokyo, and checking its sprawl, could be undertaken, to 'solve' problems created by the 'overconcentration' of population and industry. The principles involved were strictly those of the earlier Abercrombie plan for London : a built-up ring of the city was identified; a surrounding green belt, 12 kilometres wide, was proposed (although the planning powers provided have not proved strong enough to preserve it); and beyond the green belt, new towns were proposed to accommodate additional metropolitan growth. This legislation proved ineffective, however. To provide additional powers, a 1962 law concerning the construction of New Industrial Cities provided a mechanism for guiding industry into smaller towns, to complement the 1959 Law Restricting Industrial and Educational Estabments in Built-Up Areas of the National Capital Region.

Later, a U.N. Survey Team recommended similar policies as part of a 'broader area administration' for Hanshin (Osaka–Kobe) and adjacent areas, effectuated under the Kinki Region Readjustment Law (1965). Later in 1966 the Diet passed the Chubu Region Development and Readjustment Law for Nagoya. However, a policy contradiction developed, for the accelerated economic development plans of the state produced accelerated concentration of economic activity hypersensitive to international markets at the time that plans were being made for population dispersal. To attempt to remove the contradiction, under the provision of the New Industrial City Development Promotion Law, sixteen new towns were planned for Hokkaido, Tohoku, Chubu, Chugoka, Shikoku and Kyushu. Little has come of this, however, because of the competitive attitude of local governments with respect to economic development. There was a clear need for concerted action at the national level.

This came in the late 1960s with the New Comprehensive National Development Programme, the purpose of which is to place a national development policy as an overlay on the plans of local authorities in the style of French planning, designating growth and non-growth areas. This action comes in an atmosphere of crisis—the feeling that local self-determination has to give way before national purpose if the scale of centralised development is not to cause Japan to founder in the sea of environmental pollution that has been produced by the laissez-faire post-war industrial and urban growth. But as yet, the issues have simply been joined. The stage has been reached in which a searching for nationwide and long-range development policy is taking place. In the past the Japanese process of urbanisation has been a unique blend of the Western and the Oriental, involving the coexistence of industrial urbanisation and an Asian style of life. But Japan is now trying to work out an urban policy in which economic efficiency is balanced by achievement of a social organisation in which everyone is guaranteed a minimum standard of living wherever he may live, and in which he can choose his places of residence and work from among many alternatives made possible by indigenous, innovative technologies, that do not blindly adopt the assumptions and premises having their origins in the differing cultures of the West.

The Third World

Increasingly affirmative and effective planning and action is something to which all of the countries of the Third World aspire. The Third World countries constitute a diverse mosaic in which traditional self-perpetuating, self-regulating, semi-autonomous, largely pre-industrial little societies coexist with and are being changed by post-war modernisation. Traditional forms of authority and the centralised controls of colonialism have been replaced by one-party governments or military dictatorships. There is frequent instability, and limited capacity for public administration. The public sectors are small. There is fragmentation of economies along geographic, ethnic and modern-versus-traditional lines, imperfection of markets and limited development of modern economic institutions, limited industrial development and continued predominance of agriculture, low per capita product and market dependence on foreign economic relations.

Yet there is also accelerated urban growth, a compounding of the scale of the primate cities and their associated peripheral settlements, perceived increases in social pathologies, growing attachment to national urban planning as a means of securing control of social and economic change, and an increasing willingness to experiment with new and radical plans and policies. The countries of the Third World are reaching for powers, controls and planning best exemplified by the welfare states of Western Europe on the side of innovative planning, and by the command economies of Eastern Europe and the U.S.S.R. in the sense of more complete and effective controls. At the same time many are seeking to preserve significant elements of their traditional cultures, so that modernisation and westernisation are not synonymous in such cases.

The Redistributive Welfare States of Western Europe

The radicalism of the welfare states of western Europe is one that involves the modification of the free enterprise system and its larger-scale twentieth-century heirs by governmental action to reduce social and spatial inequities and to provide every citizen with minimum guarantees for material welfare—medical care, education, employment, housing and pensions. This is usually achieved through differential taxation and welfare payments, but it also involves associated extensions of more centralised decision-making designed to make the market system satisfy social goals in addition to its traditional economic functions. In this way, what has emerged are modified or mixed capitalist economies, the hallmarks of which are pluralistic societies with multiparty governments, relatively high levels of development and per capita output, built-in capacity for continued growth, and substantial public sectors alongside elaborate private markets and 'modern' economic institutions.

Public involvement in urbanisation is to be seen as more than merely a counterpoint to private interests in these cases. By directing society towards goals of redistribution and equity, the competitive drive is reoriented. By constructing a large share of all housing in existing towns, and by constructing new towns, the public exercises developmental leadership. Urbanisation is deliberately led in new directions.

Socialist Directions

From leadership, hoping that others will follow, the next step is to command, as in the socialist states, where monolithic governmental systems are dominated by a single party; there is state operation of non-agricultural industries (in some, agriculture, too) and centralised direction of the economy. Each of the socialist nations shows strong commitment to economic growth, but on the social side there is also elimination of most of the status differences based upon economic rewards that are the hallmark of free-enterprise competition. A greater uniformity and lack of specialisation is to be seen in the urban fabric, alongside more highly regimented life styles and building patterns. It is easier to command with an explicit set of rules and procedures to be followed; in this way urban development has been both bureaucratised and standardised under socialism.

FOUR MODES OF PLANNING

A sequence of four modes of planning may be discerned in the foregoing socio-political sequence : reactive or ameliorative problem-solving, allocative trend-modification, exploitive opportunity seeking and developmental leadership, and normative goal-orientation. These involve progressive achievement of greater closure or control with respect to both means and ends and the passage from the past to an idealised future as the determinant of the urban future. The four modes are described in Table 8 and depicted in Fig. 18. As will now be demonstrated, however, they are all variants of the more general policy model diagrammed in Fig. 17.

The general model may be understood if one distinguishes between two categories of *inputs* (external forces and policy instruments) that produce change in the *urban system*, resulting in two

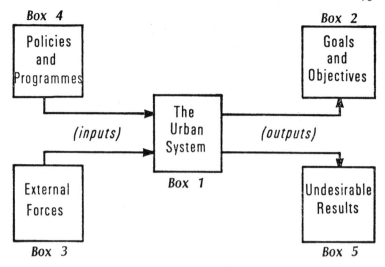

FIG. 17   An urban policy model

different types of *outputs* (undesirable results, or 'problems' and sought-after results, or 'goals'). In this way, the model may be thought of as a series of 'boxes', as in Fig. 17. In understanding the parts, we first need to consider Box 1, the 'system' to be acted upon. The urban system is composed of individuals and institutions co-existing in an environment composed of interacting natural and cultural processes, and possessing an established set of traditions or values.

Such systems are open, not closed, changed by the influences of forces from within and the impact of forces from without. Their essence is *process* not place; they are in continual motion, responsive to the dynamics of change that produce systems of heightened complexity and scale, in which interactions intensify and tensions increase. The tensions, in turn, incite the so-called urban crisis and produce 'urban problems' as one category of output.

Unfortunately, much of this change in urban systems appears to be without purpose, and without a sense of purpose there is often little satisfaction with the results and rather narrow focus on the problems. The purpose of urban policy is thus to point the polity towards goals. This is the responsibility of national and civic leadership. Such policy has to be future-oriented. It cannot remain

Table 8

Differing modes of planning

| | PLANNING FOR PRESENT CONCERNS | PLANNING FOR THE FUTURE | | |
| | Reacting to past problems | Responding to predicted futures | | Creating desired future |
	AMELIORATIVE PROBLEM-SOLVING	ALLOCATIVE TREND-MODIFYING	EXPLOITIVE OPPORTUNITY-SEEKING	NORMATIVE GOAL-ORIENTED
PLANNING MODE	*Planning for the present* Analyse problems, design interventions, allocate resources accordingly.	*Planning toward the future* Determine and make the best of trends and allocate resources in accordance with desires to promote or alter them.	*Planning with the future* Determine and make the most of trends and allocate resources so as to take advantage of what is to come.	*Planning from the future* Decide on the future *desired* and allocate resources so that trends are changed or created accordingly. Desired future may be based on present, predicted or new values.
PRESENT OR SHORT-RANGE RESULTS OF ACTIONS	*Ameliorate present problems*	*A sense of hope* New allocations shift activities	*A sense of triumphing over fate* New allocations shift activities	*A sense of creating destiny* New allocations shift activities
FUTURE OR LONG-RANGE RESULTS OF ACTIONS	*Haphazardly modify the future* by reducing the future burden and sequelae of present problems.	*Gently balance and modify the future* by avoiding predicted problems and achieving a 'balanced' progress to avoid creating major bottlenecks and new problems.	*Unbalance and modify future* by taking advantage of predicted happenings, avoiding some problems and cashing in on others without major concern for emergence of new problems.	*Extensively modify the future* by aiming for what could be. 'Change the predictions' by changing values or goals, match outcomes to desires, avoid or change problems to ones easier

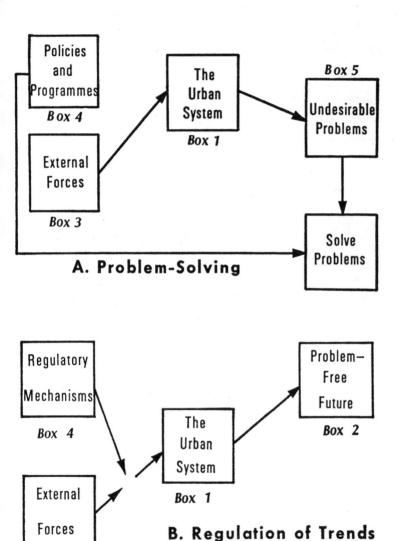

A. Problem-Solving

B. Regulation of Trends

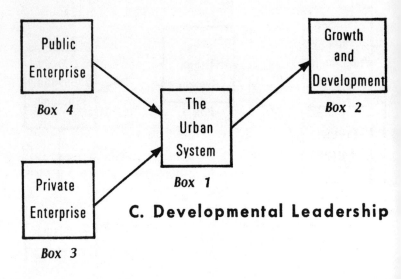

C. Developmental Leadership

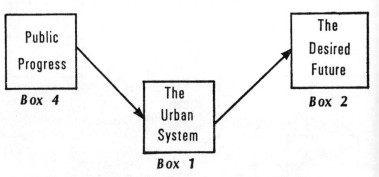

D. Goal-Oriented Planning

FIG. 18 Four urban policy-making styles

bound up with problems arising in the past, nor even with the present. It has to anticipate the future; indeed, it has to invent the future.

This brings us to Box 2 of the policy model, which contains the goals. Constructive urban policy is seen as being directed to achieving long-range goals and meeting specified objectives on the way toward the realization of these goals. But this begs a major question. Are urban systems teleological (this is purposeful)? Can they be made goals-oriented and managed by affirmative policies and planning? Or, is the urban system simply a series of existential situations or events to which, at best, the civic community will respond? Different societies have answered these questions in different ways, as we have seen, and thus have embodied into their planning process quite different versions of the policy model portrayed in Fig. 17.

Every urban system exists in a world of cultural and historical constraints. Inevitably, ideological expediency rather than political wisdom will retard development; ignorance is always aggressively available to prevent the rationalisation of the urban process. Agrarian legal systems and obsolete political structures make it difficult, if not impossible, to attain goals or even to reach temporary targets. In turn, these restrictive and restraining forces tend to inspire negative policy, aimed at preventing change from taking place. And, as a consequence, urban planning often takes on a reactive, curative role, simply responding to crises and trying to clean up 'bundles' of crises which, for want of a better term, we might call 'messes' (Box 5).

Box 3 of the model draws attention to exogenous forces—all those inputs into the system that influence its future behaviour and whose causes lie beyond the influence of the urban policy-maker, for example war, inflation, the birth rate, and behaviour of the Gross National Product. A small rise in the GNP will probably do more to increase the economic growth of a city than all the effort the planner can make to bring industry into the community. A policy maker has to be knowledgeable not only about the internal structure of his system; he also has to be thoroughly familiar with these forces from beyond the system and the nature of their energies.

Now, we can turn to the policy maker who, understanding the nature of the urban system with which he is dealing, and having some insights of the influence of external forces upon it, considers the kinds of policy which he has to put into the system to achieve the desired goals (Box 4). There appear to be three kinds of policy he can formulate : policy dealing with the social or physical environment, policy dealing with institutional structures, and policy dealing with the values established within the system. First of all, the policy maker has to determine the nature of the problem. He has to know whether he is simply to ameliorate current problems or to design an idealised alternative future. He has a range of policies at his disposal, but he has to know the types of policy to be utilised in light of the internal and external energies encountered in the workings of the system. Thus, policies become instrumental; that is, 'levers' to be 'pulled' in order to cause change in the system—change to correct a condition or to control development or to create a desired condition. Whether the policies are effective, or whether they are suppressed by more powerful external forces depends on how well the policy maker has comprehended the problem and the techniques and controls made available to him by the political actors. The policies have to be implemented with programmes, which may be effective or may not be. The best of policies are ineffective if programmed poorly.

A Sequence of Determinants of the Future

We are now at the point where we can understand the sequence of four modes of planning distinguished in Table 6 and diagrammed in Fig. 18. The most common is simply *ameliorative problem-solving*—the natural tendency to do nothing until problems arise or undesirable dysfunctions are perceived to exist in sufficient amounts to demand corrective or ameliorative action. Such 'reactive' or 'curative' planning proceeds by studying 'problems', setting standards for acceptable levels of tolerance of the dysfunctions, and devising means for scaling the problems back down to acceptable proportions. The focus is upon present problems, which implies continually reacting to processes that have already worked themselves out in the past; in a processual sense, then, such planning is past-oriented. And the implied goal is the preservation of the 'mainstream' values of the past by smoothing out the problems that arise along the way.

A second style of planning is *allocative trend-modifying*. This is the future-oriented version of reactive problem-solving. Present trends are projected into the future and likely problems are forecast. The planning procedure involves devising regulatory mechanisms to modify the trends in ways that preserve existing values into the future, while avoiding the predicted future problems. Such is Keynesian economic planning, highway building designed to accommodate predicted future travel demands, or Master Planning using the public counterpoint of zoning ordinances and building regulations.

The third planning style is *exploitive opportunity-seeking*. Analysis is performed not to identify future problems, but to seek out new growth opportunities. The actions that follow pursue those opportunities most favourably ranked in terms of returns arrayed against feasibility and risk. Such is the entrepreneurial world of corporate planning, the real-estate developer, the industrialist, the private risk-taker—and also of the public entrepreneur acting at the behest of private interests, or the national leader concerned with exercising *developmental leadership*, as when Ataturk built Ankara, or as the Brazilians are developing Amazonia today. It is in this latter context in already-developed situations that the concept of strategy planning, discussed earlier, was developed.

Finally, the fourth mode of planning involves explicitly *normative goal-orientation*. Goals are set, based upon images of the desired future, and policies are designed and plans implemented to guide the system towards the goals, or to change the existing system if it cannot achieve the goals. This style of planning involves the cybernetic world of the systems analyst, and is only possible when a society can achieve closure of means and ends; i.e. acquire sufficient control and coercive power to ensure that inputs will produce desired outputs.

The four different planning styles have significantly different long-range results, ranging from haphazard modifications of the future produced by reactive problem-solving, through gentle modification of trends by regulatory procedures to enhance existing values, to significant unbalancing changes introduced by entrepreneurial profit-seeking, to creation of a desired future specified *ex ante*. Clearly, in any country there is bound to be some mixture of all styles present, but equally, predominant value systems so determine the preferred policy-making and planning style that significantly different processes assume key roles in determining the future in different societies.

The publicly supported private developmental style that characterises the American scene, incorporating bargaining among major
interest groups, serves mainly to protect developmental interests
by reactive or regulatory planning, ensuring that the American
urban future will be a continuation of present trends, only changing as a result of the impact of change produced by the exploitive
opportunity-seeking planning of American corporations.

On the other hand, hierarchical social and political systems,
where the governing class is accustomed to govern, where other
classes are accustomed to acquiesce, and where private interests
have relatively less power, can more readily evolve urban and
regional growth policies at the national level than systems under
the sway of the market, local political jurisdictions, or egali-
tarian political processes (Rodwin, 1970). This is one reason urban
growth policies burgeoned earlier in Britain than in the United
States. Controls are of several kinds. Most basically, use of the
land is effectively regulated in conformity to a plan that codi-
fies some public concept of the desirable future and welcomes
private profit-seeking development only to the extent that it con-
forms to the public plan. Such is the underpinning of urban development in Britain, in Sweden, in France, in the Netherlands,
in Israel's limited privately owned segments or within the designated White areas of South Africa. Such a situation also obtains,
it might be added, in the planning of Australia's new capital,
Canberra. To understand the developmental outcome in these
circumstances, one must understand the aspirations of private
developers or of public agencies involved in the development process on the one hand, and the images of the planners built into
the Master Plan on the other. It is the resolution of the two forces
that ultimately shapes the urban scene. In Britain, Cherry (1972)
has concluded that the planners' images of the desirable future
have been essentially conservative, aiming to project into the
future a belief that centrality is an immutable necessity for urban
order, leading to the preservation of urban forms that are fast
vanishing in North America. In Chapter 4, we noted the differences in concept between British and European New Towns programmes. What these differences highlight is the importance of the
utopian image that becomes embedded in the specific plan and
the efficacy with which the public counterpoint functions to con-
strain private interests.

Nowhere has the imagery of the social reformers of the nineteenth century been more apparent than in Soviet planning for the 'city of socialist man'. Reflecting the reactions against the human consequences of nineteenth-century industrial urbanisation, the public counterpoint of the 'mixed' economies has been replaced by the goal-oriented planning of the socialist states and other directed societies. If, to understand urbanisation and its consequences in the mixed economies, one has to understand the nature and resolution of private and public forces, in directed societies one has to understand national goals and the ideologies of the planners, for the most important fact of the past quarter-century has been the realisation that such sought-after futures can be made to come true.

Adna Weber concluded that the history of attempts to change the nature of urbanisation was, to his day, a history of failure. Today we must conclude differently. Images of the desirable future are becoming major determinants of that future in societies that are able to achieve closure between means and ends. Political power is thus becoming a major element of the urbanisation process. Combined with the will to plan and an image of what might be, it can be directed to produce new social forms and outcomes, making it possible for a society to create what it believes *should be* rather than extending what *is* or what *has been* into the future.

References and Works Cited

P. ABERCROMBIE, *Greater London Plan 1944* (H.M.S.O., 1945).

C. ABRAMS, *Man's Struggle for Shelter in an Urbanising World* (The M.I.T. Press, 1964).

J. L. ABU-LUGHOD, *Cairo* (Princeton University Press, 1971).

———— 'Migration Adjustments to City Life: The Egyptian Case', *American Journal of Sociology*, 67 (1961) 22–32.

———— *The City is Dead, Long Live the City* (Berkeley, University of California C.P.D.R. Monograph 12, 1968).

J. ADDAMS, *Twenty Years at Hull House* (New American Library, 1961).

W. ALONSO, 'What Are New Towns For?', *Urban Studies*, 7 (1970) 37–55.

C. ANDERSON, *White Protestant Americans* (Prentice-Hall, 1970).

D. J. ARMOR, 'The Evidence on Busing', *The Public Interest*, No. 28 (1972) 90–126.

J. L. ARNOLD, *The New Deal in the Suburbs. A History of the Greenbelt Town Program* (Ohio State University Press, 1971).

W. ASHWORTH, *Genesis of Modern British Town Planning* (Routledge & Kegan Paul, 1954).

K. ASTRÖM, *City Planning in Sweden* (The Swedish Institute, 1967).

E. C. BANFIELD, *The Unheavenly City* (Little, Brown, 1968).

BARLOW REPORT, *Report of the Royal Commission on the Distribution of Industrial Population*, Cmd. 6153 (H.M.S.O., 1940).

R. P. BECKINSALE and J. M. HOUSTON, *Urbanisation and Its Problems* (Basil Blackwell, 1968).

D. BELL, 'The Measurement of Knowledge and Technology', in *Indicators of Social Change*, ed. B. Sheldon and W. E. Moore (The Russell Sage Foundation, 1968).

E. BELLAMY, *Looking Backward, 2000–1887* (Houghton, Mifflin, 1888).

P. L. VON DER BERGHE, 'Distance Mechanisms in Stratification', *Sociology and Social Research*, 44 (1960) 155–64.

B. J. L. BERRY, 'City Size and Economic Development', in *Urban-*

ization and National Development, ed. L. Jakobson and V. Prakash (Sage Publications, 1971).

P. BLAKE, *Le Corbusier* (Baltimore, Penguin Books, 1966).

C. BOOTH, *Life and Labour of the People of London* (Macmillan, 1902–3).

G. BREESE, *Urbanization in Newly-Developing Countries* (Prentice-Hall, 1966).

A. BRIGGS, *Victorian Cities* (Odhams, 1963).

E. M. BRUNER, 'Urbanization and Ethnic Identity in Northern Sumatra', *American Anthropologist,* 63 (1961) 508.

E. BRUTZKUS, *Physical Planning in Israel* (Jeursalem, by the author, 1964).

G. L. BURKE, *Greenheart Metropolis: Planning the Western Netherlands* (Macmillan, 1966).

G. E. CHERRY, *Urban Change and Planning* (G. T. Foulis, 1972).

F. CHOAY, *L'Urbanisme, Utopie et Réalities* (Paris, Senil, 1965).

P. H. CHOMBART DE LAUWE, *Paris et l'Agglomération Parisienne* (Presses Universitaires de France, 1952).

C. CLARK, *Population Growth and Land Use* (Macmillan, 1967).

M. B. CLINARD, *Slums and Community Development* (The Free Press, 1966).

E. COHEN, *The City in the Zionist Ideology* (Center for Urban Studies, Hebrew University, 1970).

COMMISSION ON POPULATION GROWTH AND THE AMERICAN FUTURE, *Population and the American Future* (U.S. Government Printing Office, 1972).

C. H. COOLEY, *Human Nature and the Social Order* (Scribner's, 1902).

P. K. CONKIN, *Tomorrow a New World: The New Deal Community Program* (American Historical Association, by Cornell University Press, 1959).

W. A. CORNELIUS, JR, 'The Political Sociology of Cityward Migration in Latin America', in *Latin American Urban Research,* ed. F. F. Rabinowitz and F. M. Trueblood, vol. 1 (Sage Publications, 1971).

P. COWAN *et al., The Office: A Facet of Urban Growth* (Heinemann, 1969).

R. J. CROOKS, 'Urbanization and Social Change : Transitional Urban Settlements in the Developing Countries', *Rehovot Conference Papers* (Rehovot, Settlement Study Center, 1971).

J. DAHIR, *The Neighborhood Unit Plan* (Russell Sage Foundation, 1947).

K. DAVIS, *World Urbanization, 1950–70* (Berkeley, University of California, 1969).

C. Delgado, 'Three Proposals Regarding Accelerated Urbanization Problems in Metropolitan Areas: The Lima Case', in *Latin American Urban Policies and the Social Sciences*, ed. J. Miller and R. Gakenheimer (Sage Publications, 1969).

B. P. Dewitt, *The Progressive Movement* (New York, The Macmillan Co., 1915).

R. E. Dickinson, *The West European City* (Routledge & Kegan Paul, 1957).

A. Dotson, 'The Role of Urban Development in National Government' (Keynote Address, Urban Development Workshop, U.S. Agency for International Development, 1972).

Y. Dror, *Public Policymaking Re-examined* (Chandler, 1968).

É. Durkheim, *De la Division du Travail Social* (Alcan, 1893).

D. J. Dwyer (ed.), *The City as a Centre of Change in Asia* (Hong Kong University Press, 1972).

T. H. Elkins, *The Urban Explosion* (Macmillan, 1973).

F. Engels, *The Condition of the English Working Classes in 1844* (Allen & Unwin, 1962 ed.).

———— *The Housing Question* (International Publishers, 1935 ed.).

L. A. Eyre, 'The Shantytowns of Montego Bay, Jamaica', *The Geographical Review*, 62 (1972) 394–413.

T. J. D. Fair, 'Southern Africa : Bonds and Barriers in a Multi-Racial Region', in *A Geography of Africa*, ed. R. M. Prothero (Routledge & Kegan Paul, 1969).

S. F. Fava, *Urbanism in World Perspective* (Thomas Y. Crowell Co., 1968).

A. Fein, *Frederick Law Olmsted and the American Environmental Tradition* (Braziller, 1972).

C. S. Fischer (a), 'The Experience of Living in Cities' (Paper prepared for a committee of the National Research Council, National Academy of Sciences, 1972).

———— (b), 'Urbanism as a Way of Life : A Review and an Agenda', *Sociological Methods and Research*, 1 (1972) 187–242.

J. C. Fisher (ed.), *City and Regional Planning in Poland* (Cornell University Press, 1966).

———— 'Planning the City of Socialist Man', *Journal of the American Institute of Planners*, vol. 28, no. 4 (1962) 251–65.

D. L. Foley, *Controlling London's Growth* (Berkeley, University of California, 1963).

B. J. Frieden and R. Morris, *Urban Planning and Social Policy* (Basic Books, 1968).

E. A. Friedmann, 'The Impact of Aging on the Social Structure',

Handbook of Social Gerontology ed. C. Tibbits (University of Chicago Press, 1960).

J. FRIEDMANN and J. MILLER, 'The Urban Field', *Journal of the American Institute of Planners*, 31 (1965) 312–19.

———— and F. SULLIVAN, 'The Absorption of Labor in the Urban Economy : The Case of Developing Economies' (Los Angeles, University of California, School of Architecture and Planning, 1972).

O. R. GALLE, W. R. GOVE and J. M. McPHERSON, 'Population Density and Pathology : What Are the Relations For Man?' *Science*, 176 (1970) 23–30.

H. J. GANS, *The Urban Villagers* (The Free Press of Glencoe, 1962).

———— *The Levittowners* (Pantheon, 1967).

———— *People and Plans* (Basic Books, 1968).

P. GEDDES, *Cities in Evolution* (rev. ed., Williams & Norgate, 1949).

C. GEERTZ, *Peddlers and Princes* (University of Chicago Press, 1963).

R. GLASS (ed.), *London: Aspects of Change* (MacGibbon & Kee, 1961).

N. GLAZER and D. P. MOYNIHAN, *Beyond the Melting Pot* (The M.I.T. Press, 1963).

P. G. GOHEEN, *Victorian Toronto* (Department of Geography Research Paper, University of Chicago, 1970).

S. GOLDSTEIN and C. GOLDSCHEIDER, *Jewish Americans* (Prentice-Hall, 1968).

M. M. GORDON, *Assimilation in American Life* (New York, Oxford University Press, 1964).

J. GOTTMANN, *Megalopolis* (The Twentieth Century Fund, 1961).

S. GREER, *The Emerging City* (The Free Press, 1962).

———— (ed.), *The New Urbanization* (St. Martin's Press, 1968).

———— *The Urbane View* (New York, Oxford University Press, 1972).

P. HALL, *The World Cities* (World University Press, 1966).

O. HANDLIN and J. BURCHARD (eds.), *The Historian and the City* (Harvard University Press, 1963).

W. J. and J. L. HANNA, *Urban Dynamics in Africa* (Aldine, 1971).

J. HARDOY, 'Urbanization Policies and Urban Reform in Latin America', in F. F. Rabinowitz and F. M. Trueblood (eds.), *Latin American Urban Research*, vol. 2 (Sage Publications, 1972).

C. D. HARRIS, *Cities of the Soviet Union* (Rand McNally, 1970).

A. HARRISON, *The Framework of Economic Activity: The International Economy and the Rise of the State* (Macmillan, 1968).

P. M. HAUSER and L. F. SCHNORE (eds.), *The Study of Urbanization* (John Wiley & Sons, 1965).

J. HAUTREUX and M. ROCHEFORT 'Les métropoles et la fonction régionale dans l'armature urbaine française', *Revue Construction et Aménagement*, no. 17 (1964) 38 pp.

B. J. HERAUD, 'Social Class and the New Towns', *Urban Studies*, 5 (1968) 33–58.

L. HOLZNER, 'Soweto-Johannesburg', *Geographische Rundschau*, 23–6 (1971) 209–22.

E. M. HOOVER and R. VERNON, *Anatomy of a Metropolis* (Harvard University Press, 1959).

E. HOWARD, *Garden Cities of Tomorrow* (Faber & Faber, 1902).

F. C. HOWE, *The City: The Hope of Democracy* (Charles Scribner's Sons, 1905).

M. JANOWITZ, *The Community Press in an Urban Setting* (The Free Press, 1952).

M. JEFFERSON, 'The Law of the Primate City', *Geographical Review*, 29 (1939) 226–32.

M. JUPPENLATZ, *Cities in Transformation. The Urban Squatter Problem of the Developing World* (Univ. of Queensland Press, 1970).

B. S. KHOREV and D. G. KHODZHAYEV, 'The Conception of a Unified System of Settlement and the Planned Regulation of City Growth in the USSR', *Soviet Geography*, 8 (1972) 90–8.

H. H. L. KITANO, *Japanese Americans* (Prentice-Hall, 1969).

P. T. KIVELL, 'A Note on Metropolitan Areas, 1961–71', *Area*, vol. 4, no. 3 (1972) 179–84.

J. G. KOHL, *Der Verkehr und die Ansiedlung der Menschen* (Arnoldische Buchhandlung, 1841).

F. S. KRISTOF, 'Federal Housing Policies : Subsidized Production, Filtration and Objectives', *Land Economics*, 48 (1972) 309–20.

I. KRISTOL, An Urban Civilization without Cities', *The Washington Post Outlook* (3 December 1972).

S. KUZNETS, *Modern Economic Growth* (Yale University Press, 1966).

J. B. LANSING, R. W. MARANS and R. B. ZEHNER, *Planned Residential Environments* (Ann Arbor, Institute for Social Research, 1970).

A. A. LAQUIAN (ed.), *Rural-Urban Migrants and Metropolitan Development* (Intermet, 1971).

———— *Slums are for People* (Manila, College of Public Administration, 1969).

R. LAWTON, 'An Age of Great Cities', *Town Planning Review*, 43 (1972) 199–224.

E. Leacock (ed.), *Culture and Poverty* (Simon & Schuster, 1971).

J. Le Corbusier, *Concerning Town Planning* (The Architectural Press, 1947).

J. W. Lewis, *The City in Communist China* (Stanford University Press, 1971).

O. Lewis, *Five Families: Mexican Case Studies in the Culture of Poverty* (Basic Books, 1959).

————— *La Vida* (Vintage Books, 1968).

E. Lichtenberger, 'The Nature of European Urbanism', *Geoforum*, no. 4 (1970) pp. 45–62.

C. E. Lindbloom, 'The Science of Muddling Through', in *Politics and Social Life*, ed. N. W. Polsby (Houghton Mifflin, 1963).

N. H. Lithwick, *Urban Canada* (Ottawa, Central Mortgage and Housing Corporation, 1970).

K. Little, *West African Urbanization* (Cambridge University Press, 1965).

P. C. Lloyd, *Africa in Social Change* (New York, Penguin Books, 1967).

R. Lubove, *The Urban Community* (Prentice-Hall, 1967).

Sir Frederick J. D. Lugard, *The Dual Mandate in British Tropical Africa* (W. Blackwood & Sons, 1920).

A. Mabogunje, *Urbanisation in Nigeria* (University of London Press, 1968).

Sir Henry Maine, *Ancient Law* (Murray, 1861).

W. Mangin, 'Latin American Squatter Settlements', *Latin American Research Review*, 2 (1967) 65–98.

R. W. Marans and W. Rodgers, 'Toward an Understanding of Community Satisfaction' (Paper prepared for the National Academy of Sciences, National Research Council, 1972).

P. Marris, 'African City Life'. *Nakanga One* (Kampala, Uganda, Transition Books, 1967).

D. C. McClelland, *The Achieving Society* (Van Nostrand, 1961).

T. G. McGee 'Catalysts or Cancers : The Role of Cities in Asian Society', in *Urbanization and National Development*, ed. L. Jakobson and V. Prakash (Sage Publications, 1971).

————— *The Southeast Asian City* (G. Bell & Sons, 1967).

————— *The Urbanisation Process in the Third World* (G. Bell & Sons, 1967).

R. L. Meier, *A Communications Theory of Urban Growth* (The M.I.T. Press, 1962).

P. Merlin, *New Towns* (Methuen, 1969).

W. Michelson, *Man and His Urban Environment* (Addison-Wesley, 1970).

S. MILGRAM, 'The Experience of Living in Cities', *Science*, 167 (1970).

E. MILLS, *Urban Economics* (Scott Foresman, 1972).

H. MINER (ed.), *The City in Modern Africa* (Frederick A. Praeger, 1967).

J. W. MOORE, *Mexican Americans* (Prentice-Hall, 1970).

D. P. MOYNIHAN, *Toward a National Urban Policy* (Basic Books, 1970).

L. MUMFORD, *The Urban Prospect* (Harcourt, Brace, 1956).

NATIONAL RESOURCES COMMITTEE, *Our Cities. Their Role in the National Economy* (U.S. Government Printing Office, 1937).

J. NELSON, 'The Urban Poor : Disruption or Political Integration in Third World Cities', *World Politics*, 22 (1970) 398.

F. J. OSBORN and A. WHITTICK, *The New Towns: The Answer to Megalopolis* (L. Hill, 1969).

R. J. OSBORN, 'How the Russians Plan Their Cities', *Trans-Action*, 3 (1966) 25–30.

V. PACKARD, *A Nation of Strangers* (David McKay, 1972).

R. E. PAHL, *Patterns of Urban Life* (Longman, 1970).

R. E. PARK, *Human Communities: The City and Human Ecology* (The Free Press, 1952).

——— *Society* (The Free Press, 1955).

R. E. PARK, E. W. BURGESS and R. D. MCKENZIE, *The City* (University of Chicago Press, 1925).

V. PEREVEDENTSEV, Comments reported in *Current Digest of the Soviet Press*, 21, no. 9 (1972) 8.

C. PERRY, *Housing for the Machine Age* (Russell Sage Foundation, 1939).

H. W. PFAUTZ (ed.), *Charles Booth on the City* (University of Chicago Press, 1967).

A. PINKNEY, *Black Americans* (Prentice-Hall, 1969).

Z. PIORO, M. SAVK and J. FISHER, 'Socialist City Planning : A Reexamination', *Journal of the American Institute of Planners*, 31 (1965) 31–42.

R. POETHIG, 'Life Style of the Urban Poor and Peoples' Organization', *Ekistics*, 34 (1972) 104–7.

H. M. PROSHANSKY *et al.*, *Environmental Psychology* (Holt, Rinehart & Winston, 1970).

J. QUANDT, *From the Small Town to the Great Community* (Rutgers University Press, 1970).

L. RAINWATER, *Behind Ghetto Walls* (Aldine, 1970).

R. REDFIELD, *Folk Culture of Yucatan* (University of Chicago Press, 1941).

R. REDFIELD, *Peasant Society and Culture: An Anthropological Approach to Civilization* (University of Chicago Press, 1956).
——— *Primitive World and its Transformations* (Cornell University Press, 1953).

A. J. REISS, JR, (ed.), *Louis Wirth on Cities and Social Life* (University of Chicago Press, 1964).

L. REISSMAN, *The Urban Process* (The Free Press, 1964).

L. G. REYNOLDS, *The Three Worlds of Economics* (Yale University Press, 1971).

B. T. ROBSON, *Urban Analysis* (Cambridge University Press, 1969).

L. RODWIN, *Nations and Cities* (Houghton Mifflin, 1970).

A. A. SAID (ed.), *Protagonists of Change. Subcultures in Development and Revolution* (Prentice-Hall, 1971).

M. SANTOS, *Les Villes du Tiers Monde* (Paris, Éditions M-Th. Génin, 1971).

A. S. SCHACHAR, 'Israel's Development Towns. Evaluation of a National Urbanization Policy', *Journal of the American Institute of Planners*, 37 (1971) 362–72.

M. SCOTT, *American City Planning Since 1890* (Berkeley, The University of California Press, 1969).

J.-J. SERVAN-SCHREIBER, *The American Challenge* [*Le Défi américain*] (Paris, Denoël, 1967).

G. SIMMEL, *Die Grosstädte und das Geistesleben*, in *Die Grosstadt*, ed. T. Petermann (Zahn & Jaensch, 1903).

G. SJOBERG, 'Cities in Developing and in Industrial Societies : A Cross-Cultural Analysis', in *The Study of Urbanization*, ed. P. M. Hauser and L. F. Schnore (John Wiley & Sons, 1967).
——— *The Pre-Industrial City* (The Free Press, 1960).

N. J. SMELSER, *Social Change in the Industrial Revolution* (University of Chicago Press, 1959).

L. SROLE, 'Urbanization and Mental Health : Some Reformulations', *The American Scientist*, 60 (1972) 576–83.
——— *et al.*, *Mental Health in the Metropolis* (McGraw-Hill, 1962).

M. STALLEY, *Patrick Geddes* (Rutgers University Press, 1972).

A. L. STRONG, *Planned Urban Environments* (The Johns Hopkins University Press, 1971).

W. G. SUMNER, *Folkways* (Ginn, 1906).

G. D. SUTTLES, 'Community Design' (Paper prepared for the National Research Council, National Academy of Sciences, 1972).
——— *The Social Construction of Communities* (The University of Chicago Press, 1972).

G. D. SUTTLES, *The Social Order of the Slum* (University of Chicago Press, 1968).

K. E. and A. F. TAEUBER, *Negroes in Cities* (Aldine, 1965).

R. THOMAS, *London's New Towns* (P.E.P., 1969).

H. TISDALE, 'The Process of Urbanization', *Social Forces*, 20 (1942) 311–16.

F. TÖNNIES, *Gemeinschaft und Gesellschaft* (Fues's Verlag, 1887).

M. TREBOUS, *Migration and Development* (Paris, Development Centre of O.E.C.D., 1968).

J. F. C. TURNER, *Uncontrolled Urban Settlement: Problems and Policies* (United Nations, New York, Department of Economics and Social Affairs, 1968).

———— and R. FICHTER, *Freedom to Build* (New York, The Macmillan Co., 1972).

R. TURNER, *India's Urban Future* (Berkeley, University of California Press, 1962).

D. TURNHAM and I. JAEGER, *The Employment Problem in Less Developed Countries* (Paris, Development Centre of O.E.C.D., 1971).

C. VALENTINE, *Culture and Poverty. Critique and Counterproposals* (University of Chicago Press, 1968).

R. VAUGHAN, *The Age of Great Cities* (Jackson & Walford, 1843).

G. WALLAS, *The Great Society. A Psychological Analysis* (New York, The Macmillan Co., 1914).

D. WARD, *Cities and Immigrants* (Oxford University Press, 1971).

S. B. WARNER, JR, *The Private City* (University of Pennsylvania Press, 1968).

———— *The Urban Wilderness* (Harper & Row, 1972).

M. L. WAX, *Indian Americans* (Prentice-Hall, 1971).

M. M. WEBBER, 'Order in Diversity : Community Without Propinquity', in *Cities and Space*, ed. L. Wingo (Johns Hopkins University Press, 1963) 23–56.

A. F. WEBER, *The Growth of Cities in the Nineteenth Century* (New York, The Macmillan Co., 1899).

M. WEBER, *The City* (The Free Press, 1958).

———— *Wirtschaft und Gesellschaft* (Tübingen : Mohr-Siebeck, 1922).

H. G. WELLS, *Anticipations. The Reaction of Mechanical and Scientific Progress on Human Life and Thought* (London, Harper & Row, 1902).

M. and L. WHITE, *The Intellectual Versus the City* (Harvard University Press, 1962).

W. A. WHYTE, JR, *The Organization Man* (Doubleday, 1956).

R. H. WIEBE, *The Search for Order* (Hill & Wang, 1967).

D. F. Wilcox, *The American City. A Problem in Democracy* (New York, Macmillan, 1904.)

P. Willmott, *The Evolution of a Community* (Routledge & Kegan Paul, 1963).

———— and M. Young, *Family and Class in a London Suburb* (Routledge & Kegan Paul, 1960).

L. Wirth, 'Urbanism as a Way of Life', *American Journal of Sociology*, xliv (1938) 1–24.

World Bank, *Urbanization* (Washington, D.C., I.B.R.D., 1972).

F. L. Wright, *Architecture and Modern Life* (Longmans, Green, 1932).

———— *The Living City* (Horizon Press, 1958).

T. Yazaki, *Social Change and the City in Japan* (San Francisco, Japan Publications, 1968).

R. K. Yin (ed.), *The City in the Seventies* (F. E. Peacock, 1972).

M. Young and P. Willmott, *Family and Kinship in East London* (Penguin Books, 1957).

R. B. Zehner, 'Neighborhood and Community Satisfaction in New Towns and Less Planned Suburbs', *Journal of the American Institute of Planners*, 37 (1971) 379–85.

Index